# The Archangel Experiment:

*Elevate your Relationship with the Divine*

**Stacey Brown**

*The Black Feather Intuitive*

ISBN: 978-0-9984835-0-4
(Black Feather Intuition)

For all seekers craving complete connection.

*This book came into being for you.*

*For Bear & Dmitri*

# TABLE OF CONTENTS

# Acknowledgments

To my husband, Carey, for supporting me in all ways while writing this book. For the brainstorming, the *muggle* perspective, the exacting insight that inspires creative clarity every single time. I'm truly grateful to have you in my life! Love.

To my loving mother-in-law, and the best damn cheerleader I know – Barb Parker! Where others fail, you pick up the gauntlet and exceed expectation! Thank you for being there, cheering enthusiastically! I'm so very humbled and grateful!

To my ever faithful editor and muse, Elizabeth Rouse. I do not have the words to adequately convey how lacking my life would be without you in it. Thank you for your endless support, encouragement, perspective, and spiritual butt kicking! This book is at its best because of you.

To my Bestie, Kylee Remington, for your curiosity and genuine interest in every new "hoobidie-floob" project my journey hands out! Your insights on the rough draft of this book boosted my wavering author confidence! Though we are hundreds of miles away, our hearts are one.

To Syntheia Finklepott, the best Fairy friend a girl could have! You always have by back. When this book goes viral, it'll be because you have shouted my praises from the rooftops. I'm so grateful for your unwavering belief in me, and for keeping my fairy hair glowing!

To my amazing Orin Book Club Sisters, Marianne Mello, Roe DeMattia & Susan Hall, who are always up for a serious angel discussion! I have no doubt it is because of our monthly gatherings, this book was ultimately inspired. Thank you so much for being your awesome selves!

To my WPN Crabtree sisters (Donna May, Eileen Batson, Heidi Beaudoin, Jessica Yee, Kyla Knox, Tammy Cordes, Vicki Clark Winstead, Brooke Burns Swindle) for all your amazing support, suggestions, and enthusiasm, about this latest book. Thank you for believing in me in such a heartfelt way! I'm so excited and honoured to be a part of your wonderful community. Here's to year 2!

To Andrew Lukonis, for giving me this book's title. Angels come in various forms when they have a message to deliver. Thanks for being an angel that day!

To Laura John, for another amazing book cover, and Matt Demers for beautiful meditation music! Your creative hearts shine through and I'm honoured that you continue to grace my life! Thank you from your old Crazy Voice Teacher! ;)

To my Divine Dream Team, without whom this book would not be. Though I could use a little more sleep on the regular, (hint, hint!), I'm so honoured that you choose me as an open vessel to get your guidance out to the world! Thank you for answering my need to deepen our relationships and providing the means to do so! Sending you a handful of beautiful blue butterflies your way in gratitude!

## Why The Archangels?

I don't sleep much these days. They come to me in dreams. I guess that's why I've lovingly nicknamed them my Divine Dream Team. My DDT consists of my Divine Spirit, Mother Earth, powers that be in the Universe, Ascended Masters, Archangels, Highest Guides, Creature Teachers, Elementals and LOIS (Loved Ones in Spirit). And they always have a lot to say!

Earlier this year I received several messages encouraging me to really get to know my Archangels. I bought multiple books (Doreen Virtue, Edgar Casey, Stewart Pearce to name a few) and read everything I could find. After each book, I was left wanting. While I had learned the basics – history, origins, general traits, (ad nauseum, as every book included them) - I was no closer to getting to know the Archangels in a personal way. So I went on a seminar and workshop hunt for an advanced archangel experience that was either local and affordable, or online and affordable. I came up empty.

A few months ago, my book club friends invited me to a local angel workshop happening the following weekend. The workshop description promised a program that was for advanced hoobidie-floobs (my word for all things metaphysical) as well as for beginners. "Oh the synchronicity! ... Maybe this was the workshop I'd been looking for, falling right into my lap!" I had high hopes. Well folks, I attended the workshop, and while it was well done and an enjoyable time spent with friends, I didn't learn anything new or different. I did not have a personal experience with my Archangels. I went home disappointed and resigned to the fact that what I was looking for doesn't exist.

3:33 am that morning they woke me, as they often do: "You need to write the workshop you want to attend." And for the next 2 hours, I frantically wrote down what they were giving - the outline that is now this book!

- I craved an intimate friendship and partnership with each of my Archangels.
- I wanted to know who to call on for specific needs.
- I wanted to understand *their* purpose, their needs, goals and desires because it's not all about me!!
- And most of all, I wanted to be taken to the next level on my spiritual journey, to expand my gifts in a powerfully tangible, verifiable way.

After years of driving myself batty trying to learn everything in a mainstream, traditional way (memorization and bookwork) I finally figured out that I am an experiential learner. And learning is so much more enjoyable when it's fun! So this book is NOT a history lesson. You'll find no angel origin stories or specific details on their backgrounds. This is a book of engaging experiments, most channeled, and designed to give you the opportunity to develop a deep, uniquely personal relationship with each of the Archangels known in the metaphysical realm. Guided meditations, creative analysis, movement, hands-on craft options, and group experiments are presented here to provide a well-rounded experience for every seeker's preferred mode of receiving.

Each experiment serves as a blueprint, opening the door for further relationship development at your own pace. Try all the experiments or just the ones that appeal to you. The book can be read out of sequence or straight through. Use it as a workbook for experimentation and growth, or a reference for guidance and clarity on specific issues.

Take what works for you and leave the rest behind.

The most important thing to keep in mind here is to HAVE FUN while running your own personal Archangel Experiment!

May the force be with you!

With love and gratitude,

Stacey
*The Black Feather Intuitive*

*We hold the key to our own happiness,*
*but Angels guide us to the right doors.*

*~signsofangels.com*

*Before you walk through the doors…*

As I've already mentioned, this is not an "all about the archangels" book, however I would be doing you, the reader, and the angels a disservice if I didn't mention some basic information to guide your experiment.

## Archangelic Who's Who

Angels are Love. Pure, unadulterated, unconditional love.

So if they are all the same, all about love, then why wouldn't I just call on my guardian angel for everything?

Like the human world, angels are here with their own personal purposes and missions to fulfill. They have strengths that are specific to certain aspects, issues and events. Guardians are here to keep you safe. They are your energetic eyes and ears. They don't leave your side. They are all about YOU.

The Archangels serve a broader purpose. They are the Managers and Overseers of the Guardians, making sure that everyone is fulfilling their assignments well. They have a bird's eye view of our lives, seeing the depth and scope of our human struggles from above. They see the big picture for all of us, and know how to orchestrate and maneuver to make our manifestations happen for the highest and best of all involved.

So I *could* use my Guardian angel as my go between, but the way I see it: Why have a "middle man" when you can go straight to the source?! Hence, this book.

While each Archangel is assigned to assist with a different aspect of humanity, Love reflected through these various aspects, is at the heart of the matter. Love **is** the one true aspect. It is the ultimate goal.

But our conflicts and circumstances rarely expose themselves as such. It's more likely that we see our situation through a filter of anger, confusion, hurt, grief, fear, etc. In these instances, when we seek guidance, how do we know which Archangel to reach out to?

These Archangels have a lot of humanity on their plates to oversee! A single angel can be in charge of 4-6 unique aspects, and each of those is broken down further into smaller issues. To make things as simple as possible, I chose a single theme word that best represents the essence of their responsibilities. Then, like the "Queen of England", I gave them each their own title: "Angel of (their aspect)". ie. Archangel Uriel has been dubbed the *Angel of Truth*. You will find knowing who to seek out much easier this way. Easy peazy!

What's next?

## Archangelic Golden Rule

The angelic realm lives by one rule when interacting with humanity – Free Will! The human adventure is all about choices and the experiences those choices bring. If our Divine helpers swoop in like overprotective mothers before we've taken a first step, our lives wouldn't be much of an adventure! They need your permission before they can intervene, offer guidance, and fulfill their purpose. So you must remember to ASK for their help! People often forget this step – either through ignorance or forgetfulness – and it is so important. I have built this right into each and every experiment to avoid any oversights.

## Archangelic Invite

So how do you invite an Archangel to join your party?!

1. Identify your Intention – what information, guidance, or assistance do you need?
2. Identify your Archangel - which one handles your issue? (As mentioned, I've provided each Archangel with a keyword that makes this process easier.)
3. Create your Request
4. Ask!

Try this:

1. Identify your Intention: I'm having trouble letting go of control over my daughter's life.
2. Identify your Archangel: Control falls under Surrender, Archangel Metatron.

3. Create your Request: I want to stop being so controlling over her life. She resents me for interfering and I want to support her instead of push her away.
4. Ask: Archangel Metatron, please help me to surrender my need to control my daughter's life and allow her to make her own choices. It no longer serves me. I choose love.

Identifying your intention is key to having a successful experience with your Archangels. By clearly stating what you need, your Divine Dream Team can deliver a clear outcome or direction.

That being said, I'm a low maintenance kinda gal when it comes to this type of thing. I don't want to jump through 57,000 hoops to get what I need. I want help NOW! So if I don't have the 2-5 minutes to follow those steps, or determine the right Archangel for the job, I keep it simple. "Archangels HELP" will get their attention, and they will sort out which of them can answer my needs best! Feel free to put this into practice, when required!

On that note, a book club friend of mine, Susan, is a shining example of keeping it simple. If she has an issue with her computer, she asks the "technology angels" to help her out. If she needs a special recipe for a guest with dietary restrictions, she asks the "food angels" to provide it. If she's on the road and is in a hurry to get somewhere, she asks the "transportation angels" to clear a path. And it works EVERY time!

So don't NOT ask your Archangels for help because you aren't sure who to call. A general distress call is always received and answered – your true intention will be understood!

## Archangelic Tools

Let's talk about Imagination vs. Intuition for a moment. Imagination gets a bad rap. Once you reach the age of 10, it's treated like a dirty word. Yet that couldn't be further from the Truth. Imagination is a precursor, a gateway, merely another tool to be used to access Intuition. Many of the experiments in this book ask you how you receive information from your Archangels, and imagination is included in that list. If you find that you are only using your imagination to complete these experiments, do not be discouraged or feel you are unsuccessful. It's actually an indicator of the opposite. You *are* tuning in and connecting with your Archangels with your inner vision. So open up and imagine away!

## Archangelic Names

There's a belief among Angelologists, Channelers and the like that the proper pronunciation of an Archangel's name is crucial to accessing their true vibration. But who is to say what the proper pronunciation is? In America, we obviously translate everything into the American English pronunciation. What do they do in Russia, China or Africa? You see the problem!

So here's my two cents. Don't get too hung up on it! Find a pronunciation for each Archangel that resonates within you and stick with it. I do not believe that the Archangels, *who are anxious to be called upon*, are going to ignore the call because you emphasized the wrong syll-ah-ble!

For those who would find a starting point helpful, I've included a pronunciation guide that resonates well with me, at the end of this chapter. Due to my opera background, I tend to pronounce all things non-English, with an Italian bent. If you prefer to simply sound out the names in English, by all means, do so!

## Archangelic Acknowledgement

We humans here in 3D land are often focused on Me, Myself, and I. What is in it for ME? It's all about ME!! In the Angelic realm, part of their personal purpose is to serve and protect us as we work toward our goals throughout our lifetimes. But that doesn't mean they don't enjoy a pat on the back, an "atta boy", an acknowledgement of the effort invested in our success. No one enjoys feeling unappreciated.

I am reminded of the Genie in Disney's Aladdin as he describes his life to Aladdin. "Poof. What do you need? Poof. What do you need? Poof. What do you need?" He lives to serve but he's exhausted keeping up with all the incessant lamp rubbing and wish making he's responsible for granting! Our Archangels work hard on our behalf to help us get where we need to be. So take a minute of your time to thank them for their efforts! A little goes a long way! (I've also written this right into the experiments to promote the habit.)

One final, and important, thing to do before you begin...

In my experience, there is no substitution for having an audio version of a written meditation. I've recorded and included all guided meditations in this book as a downloadable mp3, to accompany your experiments.

There are 18 *Intentions* guided meditations, one for each Archangel.

Not every Archangel has a guided meditation for their *Experiments*. Experiments with corresponding recordings are identified with an asterisk (*), and titled according to their subject matter.

Enter this link to download before you start, and enjoy!

http://www.blackfeatherintuition.com/ArchangelExperiment/

When prompted, please enter the following:

Username: archangel

Password: blackfeather2016

Now that you have the basics, are you ready to begin your own Archangel Experiment?

Let's have at it!!

## *Pronunciation Guide: Archangels*

| | |
|---|---|
| *Archangel Ariel* | **Ah-ree-ell** |
| *Archangel Azrael* | **Az-rah-yell** |
| *Archangel Cassiel* | **Kas-see-yell** |
| *Archangel Chamuel* | **Chah-moo-ell** |
| *Archangel Gabriel* | **Gah-bree-yell** |
| *Archangel Haniel* | **Hah-knee-yell** |
| *Archangel Jeremiel* | **Dghe-re-mee-yell** |
| *Archangel Jophiel* | **Dghoh-fee-yell** |
| *Archangel Michael* | **Mee-kah-yell** |
| *Archangel Metatron* | **Met-ah-trahn** |
| *Archangel Orion* | **Oh-rhee-yuhn** |
| *Archangel Raguel* | **Rag-ooo-ell** |
| *Archangel Raphael* | **Rah-fah-yell** |
| *Archangel Raziel* | **Rah-zee-yell** |
| *Archangel Sandalphon* | **Sahn-dahl-fahn** |
| *Archangel Uriel* | **Yoo-rhee-yell** |
| *Archangel Zadkiel* | **Zahd-kee-yell** |
| *Archangel Zaphkiel* | **Zahf-kee-yell** |

All names ending in "el" are pronounced with an emphasis on the last syllable.

*All names ending in "on"* are pronounced with an emphasis on the first syllable. (I cheat with Orion. I pronounce it the American English way: Oh-rha-yahn.)

## *Materials: What you'll need*

For all experiments, you will need:

- Journal and a pen
- Yoga mat, pillow and blanket

For many experiments, you will need:

- Crafting Kit: Glue gun, Double sided tape, Scissors, Scrapbooking materials, Feathers, Stickers, Beads, Jewels, Paints and Brushes, Canvas Paper, Blank Paper, Coloured Pencils or Markers

For individual Archangels, you will also need:

<u>Cassiel</u>

- A coin
- Voice Recording Device

<u>Chamuel</u>

- Reading Glasses (Dollar Store), Pink Cellophane Paper (Dollar Store)
- Crafting Kit: Glue gun, Double sided tape, Scissors, Scrapbooking materials, Feathers, Stickers, Beads, Jewels, Paints and Brushes

<u>Gabriel</u>

- Mandala Colouring Book (or single b&w mandala)

<u>Haniel</u>

- Instrumental Crystal Bowl Music
- Water, Timer
- Instrumental Meditative Music (ie. Calm Meditation Radio Pandora)
- Clipboard, Blank Paper Stack

Jophiel

- Hand Held Mirror

Metatron

- Wise Book (A book that you read often for its wisdom)

Michael

- Sketch of a sword (from online images, colouring books, or image provided at end of chapter)
- Crafting Kit: coloured pencils or markers

Raphael

- Tea cup, saucer & loose tea leaves

Raziel

- "I don't get it!" book (A book that you have difficulty understanding or getting through)
- Sacred Geometry Artwork (online or other)
- 4 oz Glass Bottle with atomizer, Essential Oils – variety, Distilled Water, Alcohol, pourable Measuring Cup

Sandalphon

- Instrumental Meditative Music (ie. Calm Meditation Radio Pandora)

Uriel

- Candle, Lighter, Flame Retardant Container
- Blank Paper Stack

Zadkiel

- Crafting Kit: Paints and Brushes, Canvas Paper
- Oracle Deck

Zaphkiel

- Instrumental Mood Music (ie. Chill Out Radio Pandora)

## Setting the Tone*

This is the meditation I use to connect with my Arch's every day. I recommend repeating this before each Archangel session, to elevate your vibration.

Find a quiet place where you won't be disturbed. Turn off your electronics. Allow a few minutes to turn off the outside world and tune into you!

- Sit or lay back, with your spine straight, and get comfortable. Allow your arms to lay relaxed at your sides, palms facing up. Close your eyes and connect with your breath. Bring your attention to your legs and pelvic area. Breathe deeply here, and visualize or imagine a warm bubble of energy forming around your legs and pelvis.
- This warm bubble of energy rises to your navel. It changes form now. It's as if you are standing in a pool of water, ripples of energy floating out and away from you. Follow those energy waves out as far as they go. Enjoy the sensation.
- Now move your attention to your diaphragm. Gently expand your diaphragm out in front of you, while breathing in through your nose slowly. When you are full of breath, release your diaphragm quickly. Feel or imagine orbital rings of light and energy spinning all around your upper arms and shoulders.
- As you explore these vibrational shifts, take a moment to breathe in your intentions for meeting your Archangels. Filter in desires and openness. Filter in a beautiful blue-white light of loving protection, allowing only that which is 100% of the Divine into your space.

- Now move your attention to your beautiful heart. Visualize a carousel of love spinning around it, streams of loving energy looping together to form a gorgeous sphere of pink light.
- These streams of light expand up into your throat, transforming into a spinning layer of feathers. These feathers sparkle and dance Divinely in a round.
- Now visualize a small, bright, purple light piercing through your third eye, opening it wide. Its beam grows out as far as you can imagine, accessing the Divine consciousness.
- Now feel or imagine the crown of your head opening fully to the Divine. It tingles and radiates translucent white light out into the far reaches of the universe.
- Picture a lighthouse beacon inside your heart. The light is large. Move closer to the light within your heart. You notice the light gets smaller with each step, burning with an otherworldly intensity. The pulse of the light matches your heartbeat. Slip into this light and feel instantly connected to your highest self.
- Bring your attention to your right hip, close to your appendix. Imagine an elastic band of light sitting in a north-south direction. Gently pull back on that light band, feeling a subtle slingshot effect aiming for the crown of your head.
- At the crown, you feel a waterfall of shimmering light cascading down and around your body. You stand or float effortlessly in the light pooling below you, confident in your assured protection, surrounded in the love of your Divine Source. You are ready to meet your Archangels!

# Meet Your League of Luminaries … The Archangels!!

# Archangel Ariel

Angel of

MOTHER

EARTH

Helps with:

- Nature & Animal Kingdoms
- Heart-felt Peace with others
- Looking out for those we love
- Finding strength during tough times

Let's talk about Mother Earth for a minute. The ground you are standing on; the air that keeps you filled with the vibrant breath of life; the rain, leaves, flowers & produce that provide beauty and sustenance. All of Mother Earth is here to support YOU - your purpose, your dreams, your desires. And she does so without agonizing effort because that is her purpose. In the spring, seeds begin to bud and grow into plants, flowers, trees, and whatever else they are intended to become. The birds, bees, and four legged creatures come out of their winter slumber naturally, ready to take on a new cycle. And all of this happens without the need of human interference.

How does nature work so well on its own, while humanity struggles to evolve? We fail to go with the flow of life! We resist our true nature, trading it in for an ideal of what we think we *should* be, instead of who we are. Our inner strength comes from that natural flow. We need only step into the stream and let our nature do the work!

## Intentions*

Close your eyes and reconnect with your breath. Bring your breath deep into your belly, bottom of the lungs, middle of the lungs, then top of the lungs. Feel your chest cavity expanding gracefully with breath. Bring your attention to the bottoms of your feet. Imagine that you are standing in a beautiful clearing in the forest, your toes scrunching into the lush, carpet-like grass beneath your feet. Walk along the grass in circles, exploring the area around you, feeling how supported you are. To your left, a stream of sunlight shines down through the trees, illuminating a figure coming towards you. It is Archangel Ariel. She is thrilled to join you on this journey to learn more about her and how she can guide you. Open your heart to her, and repeat this intention: Hi Ariel, it's an honour to meet you! I want to get to know you better. I'd love to learn about your purpose, gifts, and form of communication with me & I'm ready to receive your guidance. Please show me the mysteries of Mother Earth in a tangible, verifiable way now. I'm so grateful you have made it so!

If you wish, take this time now to add a personal intention for this experiment.

Ariel smiles and agrees. She invites you to follow her into the forest. When you are ready, gently open your eyes, and prepare to begin your adventure!

## *Experiment*

*For the next 20 minutes, take a walk! Focus on being present and in the "now". Breathe deeply and walk heel to toe throughout the walk, bringing your attention back into the present moment when you catch yourself drifting. Be aware of the sights, sounds, smells and sensations around you. ie. Notice colour contrasts between the sky and trees. Touch leaves and tree trunks. Listen for birdcalls and insects. Notice any scents in the air. Is there a breeze? What does it feel like on your face? What does the air taste like?*

*As you connect tangibly to Mother Earth, call on Archangel Ariel to help you reflect on what you can learn from nature's cycles and behavior. How can you apply the natural ebb and flow of life itself to embrace and enhance your own INNER STRENGTH? Look for signs, symbols, feelings, inspiration - anything that comes into your experience – that reflect Ariel's guidance for you. How does she communicate with you?*

*Upon your return, take a few minutes to reflect and record your observations in your journal. How did Archangel Ariel show up for you? What did she have to share? Take time now to express gratitude to Ariel for her wisdom!*

## Feathers of Wisdom

Here are a number of ways Archangel Ariel loves to be of service!

Calling all animal lovers! Ariel loves the animals. Bring all concerns about your beloved fur, feather and gill babies her way! Ask her to ease ills, interpret issues, and send love, protection and healing their way!

Not a pet owner but have troubles with others pets? Perhaps you have issues with the neighbor's dog incessantly barking at 6 in the morning. Ariel to the rescue! Try this: Ask Ariel to soothe the dogs' nerves and quiet his cords!

Trouble with raccoons rifling through your garbage? Send Ariel to encourage them to move along!

Any gardeners out there? When you just can't seem to get your tomato plants to seed properly, gardenias to flourish, or help that sickly tree at the back of your property from losing its bark, call on Ariel. She can connect with the Devas & fairy community, send energetic healing, and even provide suggestions on what you can do physically to help your beloved flora & fauna.

# Archangel Azrael

## Angel of GRIEF

Helps with:

- Death and grief
- Comfort through transition
- Crossing over
- Support for the grieving - emotional, material, spiritual

Grief is one of the most challenging emotions humans face in their lifetime. Loss of a loved one through death, divorce or relocation are said to be in the top 5 most stressful experiences a person can have. Why is this so? We have difficulty accepting drastic, life-altering change. We miss those persons, places and things we've become attached to and built our lives around. We fear being alone and invisible/unacknowledged.

For many decades now, sociologists and psychologists have broken down the grief process into 7 different stages:

1. Shock – *Initial paralysis at hearing the bad news.*
2. Denial – *Trying to avoid the inevitable.*
3. Anger – *Frustrated outpouring of bottled-up emotion.*
4. Bargaining – *Seeking in vain for a way out.*
5. Depression – *Final realization of the inevitable.*
6. Testing – *Seeking realistic solutions.*
7. Acceptance – *Finally finding the way forward.*

(Modified Kubler-Ross Model)

Like the Tower card in a traditional Tarot deck, grief presents itself as a complete undoing of what is currently known and understood as reality. It is literally having the rug pulled out from under ones life, shattering everything it supported in its wake.

Archangel Azrael helps us pick up the proverbial pieces of our broken lives and unrealized dreams while we grieve. He stands vigil, a loyal bodyguard, patiently moving one through these stages with loving wisdom.

## Intentions*

Close your eyes and connect with your breath. Inhale and exhale slowly and deeply 5 times, allowing your breath to fill your entire body from head to toe. You are feeling warm and comfortable. Imagine that you are walking slowly along a stone path. The path is filled with beautiful white and clear quartz crystals. With each step, you feel a tingling sensation rising up through your feet, calves and thighs, filling your abdomen and chest cavity, your arms, shoulders, neck and head. You are enjoying this high frequency stroll. The crystal path eventually leads you into a lovely, peaceful flower garden, filled with brilliant tropical colours. Hummingbirds, bees and butterflies dance around one another in a festival of nectar and honey. Bright lush trees sprinkle the azure sky. As you explore this fragrant garden, touching petals and leaves of silk, velvet and papyrus, you notice the path leads to a bubbling, clear fresh water brook with a bridge. This ornate bridge is seemingly made of light, as the sun reflects off the crystal base, with a beautiful wrought iron railing. In the center, sits a bench, covered in indigo and purple morning glories. You walk onto the bridge and sit down on this bench, taking in the majesty of the place. As you look across to the other side of the bridge, you realize you cannot see anything beyond this luminescent wall of white light. You have reached a portal. As you contemplate this discovery, an image emerges from the light. It is Archangel Azrael. Invite him to join you on the bench. Repeat out loud this intention: Hi Azrael! I'm honoured to meet you! I want to get to know you better. I'd love to learn about your comforting, supportive gifts, and how you communicate with me. I'm ready to receive your guidance. Please show me how to flow through all transitions in my life compassionately, and grieve fully, in a tangible, verifiable way now.

I'm so grateful you have made it so!

If you wish, take this time now to add a personal intention for this experiment.

Azrael smiles and continues to sit next to you on the bench. When you are ready to explore his gifts, gently open your eyes.

## Experiment

*Grab your journal and a pen. For the next 20 minutes, let's explore Archangel Azrael's supportive messages for you through the power of automatic writing.*

*Choose one of the 7 stages of grief to explore. Open your journal to a fresh blank page and put your pen to the paper. Close your eyes and reconnect with Azrael's energy. Ask him to use you as a completely open conduit from the Divine realm to this one, and share his guidance that is for your highest and best in a tangible, verifiable way now. Notice how Azrael comes through for you. Do you hear, see or feel his answers? Does a word simply come to you without effort? Is your hand guided to write? Or are you using your imagination to create your statements?*

*When you are ready, allow your hand to write whatever comes to you. Don't think through this experiment. Don't judge what comes or how it happens. Just wait until you are Divinely guided, and then write. Be patient. It may take a few minutes before you fully connect. Go with the flow.*

*When you feel you've received Azrael's full message, choose another stage, start a fresh page and repeat the process.*

*At the end of this stage, start a fresh page.*

*Now reflect back on a time of grief in your past. Were you able to find a silver lining to the experience? How were you able to achieve that perspective?*

*Choose a personal grief experience you've recently had, or are having. How can you apply your previous perspective to aid your current grieving process? How can you resolve any denial or anger you may be feeling? If possible, identify which stage you are in, and ask Azrael to give you clarity, guidance and comfort to help you move forward into acceptance and peace. When you feel you've received Azrael's full message, open your eyes.*

*Upon completion, take a few minutes to reflect on the experience and record your observations in your journal. What did Azrael have to share with you about grief and loss? Do you notice any shifts in your personal healing? How did he show up for you? Take time now to express gratitude to Azrael for his loving wisdom!*

## Experiment

*Grab your journal and a pen. For the next 30 minutes, explore the stages of grief with Archangel Azrael using your breath. Sit comfortably in a chair or on your yoga mat. Close your eyes and reconnect with Azrael's energy. Invite him to gift you with his gentle, comforting wisdom as you experience the stages of grief through your life force in a tangible, verifiable way now. Allow him to support you through the process in all ways required. Notice how he shows up for you – do you hear, see or feel his presence? Do you experience a release or a shift in your emotional body? Or are you using your imagination to complete the experiment? When you are ready, open your eyes.*

*Take a moment to choose a personal grief experience to work with. This can be the loss of a person, place or object. If you are currently grieving a loss, this is an excellent example to use. If you are not currently grieving, choose a past grief experience that you can easily recall.*

*Let's talk about the breath for a minute. Everything begins and ends with breath. Without it, we cease to exist in our physical bodies. We are born into this world naturally breathing from our diaphragms (when the belly rises and falls with each inhale and exhale). At some point in our lives, usually during pre-teen or teen years, most of us switch over to a shallower, chest-focused breath; our natural healthy, relaxed, belly breathing occurs only while we sleep or are extremely relaxed. This is caused by a build-up of mental, physical, emotional stressors and other pressures from the outside world, stopping us from taking in oxygen fully and completely. We "half-breathe", robbing our bodies of needed relief and regeneration. When we enter a grieving process, it is like going through a death and rebirth ourselves. Here's what happens to your breath and body as you grieve:*

*1. Shock: At receiving the news, you have a short, quick intake of breath, which comes from your diaphragm (also known as belly breath). When this happens, your muscles tense up and the diaphragm is frozen or locked.*

*Try this now: Close your eyes and go into your grief memory to when you first heard the news of your loss. Express your shock audibly through your breath by taking a short, quick intake. Notice how and where you feel the shock. What happens to your body? Do your muscles tense? Does your breath stop? Does your heart race?*

*When ready, ask Azrael to guide you through to the next stage.*

*2. Denial: In your resistance to the news, there is very little to no breath, only clenched muscles. You are cut off from your core breath, taking air into your upper chest area only (the top of the lungs).*

*Try this now: Go into your grief memory to when you first denied the occurrence. Express your denial audibly by using statements like: "This isn't happening. He/she is not gone. I'm going to wake up and realize this is all just a dream." Notice what happens to your breath as you speak. Where do you feel the denial? Do your muscles tense? Does your breath stop? Does your heart race?*

*When ready, ask Azrael to guide you through to the next stage.*

*3. Anger: As you express your frustration and helplessness with an emotional outburst, your breath releases in choppy, short bursts. Again, you are cut off from your core breath, taking in random gasps of air into the upper chest.*

*Try this now: Go into your grief memory to when you first raged against the occurrence. Express your anger audibly by using statements like: "This isn't fair! This isn't the way it was supposed to be! Why is this happening?" Notice what happens to your breath as you speak. Where do you feel the denial? Do your muscles tense? Does your breath stop? Does your heart race?*

*When ready, ask Azrael to guide you through to the next stage.*

*4. Bargaining: While trying desperately to undo what is, by any means necessary, your breath is panicked, hurried and forceful. You somewhat engage your core and your chest, begging the Source (person, place or thing) to see reason and give you what you want.*

*Try this now: Go into your grief memory to when you made a bargain with Source to change the outcome. Express your proposal(s) audibly by using statements like: "Ok God. She's missing right now. If you bring her back to me I promise I will never take your name in vain again and I'll go to church every Sunday." Notice what happens to your breath as you speak. Where does your breath come from? Where do you feel the desperation? Do your muscles tense? Does your breath stop? Does your heart race?*

*When ready, ask Azrael to guide you through to the next stage.*

*5. Depression: As you realize there is nothing you can do to change what is, your breathing is labored. You are once again disconnected from your core breath, taking in shallow upper chest air, and exhaling (sometimes in sighs) at a slower, uneven rhythm.*

*Try this now: Go into your grief memory to when you realized there was no hope. Express your depression audibly by using statements like: "There is nothing I can do to change this. They are not coming back. My life will never be the same. How can I go on?" Notice what happens to your breath as you speak. Where does your breath come from? Where do you feel hopelessness? Do your muscles tense? Does your breath stop? Does your heart race?*

*When ready, ask Azrael to guide you through to the next stage.*

*6. Testing: Now you are trying to figure out the best way to live with this new reality. Your breath is calculated and often deliberate, released in slow sighs. You are starting to reconnect with your core as well as your chest.*

*Try this now: Go into your grief memory to when you began strategizing how to live with your new reality. Express your attempts to change audibly by using statements like: "Ok. I am going to the grocery store alone today. I did this before he came into my life, surely I can do it again.... No this is too overwhelming. I don't think I can handle this. Maybe tomorrow." Notice what happens to your breath as you speak. Where does your breath come from? Where do you feel resistance to growth? Do your muscles tense? Does your breath stop? Does your heart race?*

*When ready, ask Azrael to guide you through to the next stage.*

*7. Acceptance: As you grow forward into your new reality, your breath expands fully into your diaphragm, lower and upper lungs. There is no muscle tension, tightness or pain. You feel rejuvenated and alive. Connected with your core breath again, you feel confident that you can move on successfully, with room to grow in a new direction.*

*Try this now: Go into your grief memory to when you accepted your new reality. Express your realizations audibly by using statements like: "I'm ready to move on with my life. Yes, my life looks different – it will never be the same again. But I deserve to find happiness again. My loved one would want me to. I'm ready for what the world brings me now." Notice what happens to your breath as you speak. Where does your breath come from? What characteristics does it have – gentle, soft, strong, steady, etc.? Do your muscles tense? Does your breath stop? Does your heart race?*

*Now go back to a stage where you felt stuck or unresolved with your personal grief experience. Call in Azrael to help offer comfort and support as you work through this stage now. When you feel complete, open your eyes.*

*Take a few minutes to reflect on the experience and record your observations in your journal. What did Azrael have to share with you about your personal grief and loss? Do you notice any shifts in your personal healing? How did he show up for you? Take time now to express gratitude to Azrael for his loving wisdom!*

## Feathers of Wisdom

Archangel Azrael sometimes gets a bad rap – he is feared unnecessarily. People have referred to him as the Angel of Death, implying that he brings death to humans. This is not the case! Death is a natural part of the current physical world life-cycle. When our bodies malfunction irreparably due to dis-ease or accidents, death comes. Azrael only follows to help all involved *through the process*! He is there to help the one crossing over into their next journey, as well as those left behind on earth. He is a master of transition and guides us compassionately. We would all be wise to lean on him, rather than fear him!

Wishing to connect with LOIS?! (You know…a Loved One In Spirit!)

Try this: Repeat the Intention Setting meditation for Azrael. When you sit on the bridge this time, ask to meet with a loved one by name and invite them to join you on the bench. What messages do they have for you? What questions do you have for them?

Or if you have a grief situation that involves the loss of a place or thing instead of a person, invite that to sit with you. What messages does it have to share with you? What questions do you have for it? Ask away!

In both scenarios, don't be afraid…Azrael will be there to protect you both so enjoy the experience!

Many times when there is a death of a loved one, finances become strained: How will we be able to afford a funeral and all that entails? Our bank account has been frozen and I can't access money to live until the legal issues have been satisfied. How will I make it? My loved one was sick for so long and our medical bills have created lasting debt. How will I be able to pay that off?

Call on Azrael to help you find a way! One of his many skills includes providing Financial Support to those in grief. Thanks Azrael for taking care of me emotionally, spiritually and financially, when I'm overwhelmed and unable to!

# Archangel Cassiel

Helps with:

- Duality within each of us; Light & Dark accepted & integrated
- Creating new realities
- Sharing Divine gifts with others
- Astral Knowledge, General Occult Matters, Reincarnation
- Death & dis-ease, Psychic attack, Spirit communication, Meditation

Duality: an instance of opposition or contrast between two concepts or two aspects of something; a dualism.

This definition expertly describes a fundamental part of our human experience here on Earth. We cannot understand light without first experiencing dark (absence of light), joy without sorrow (absence of joy), in without first experiencing out (opposite of in), or up without down (opposite of up). Like two sides of a coin, one cannot exist without the other.

Herein lies an interesting paradox for our human brains to ponder, for our egos to resist. We have been taught to judge our surroundings, our experiences, our relationships as good or bad, right or wrong, happy or sad. Yet we *need* both aspects of an experience to fully integrate our ego into our high selves, healing the duality within. We need to explore both to end our suffering, accept ourselves fully just as we are, and live fearlessly in the NOW, in the present moment, in joy. We ARE both, and we are neither. Within this understanding there is Balance. Within this balance there is Harmony. Within this harmony there is Oneness. And within Oneness is Love, in every moment. And every moment is perfect, just as it is. Enter Archangel Cassiel, also known as the Angel of Tears, for true joy comes from being comforted through the tears of sorrow.

## Intentions*

Close your eyes and connect to your breath. Inhale and exhale until you find a comfortable rhythm. Clench and tighten all your muscles all at once. Hold for 3 seconds, then, release them with an audible sigh on "ah". Repeat this again. Clench and tighten all your muscles – including your jaw, forehead, stomach, and feet. Hold for 3 seconds, then release with an audible "ah". Allow your legs and arms to flop out to the sides, without any tension. Now focus on being perfectly still. Notice how your body reacts or responds to stillness. Visualize yourself sitting in a black room, in front of a full-length mirror. You are dressed in white. As you examine your reflection, you realize you are only able to see your silhouette. Only your shadow is visible, black against a white room. It is standing tall. You raise your right arm toward the mirror and your shadow raises its left, reflecting its opposite. You frown in confusion, and your shadow smiles wide with understanding. As you ponder this moment, your reflection begins to move toward you, stepping out of the mirror. You feel a very comforting presence fill the room. Tears of joy wet your eyes and you realize that Archangel Cassiel has joined you. Repeat out loud this intention: Hi Cassiel! It's an honour to meet you! I want to get to know you better. I'd love to learn about your gifts, and how you communicate with me. I'm ready to receive your guidance. Please show me how to accept and integrate all aspects of duality in my life, in a tangible, verifiable way now. I'm so grateful you have made it so!

If you wish, take this time now to add a personal intention for this experiment.

Cassiel, your shadow, takes your hand and leads you into the mirror for an adventure! When you are ready, gently open your eyes.

## *Experiment**

*Grab a coin, journal and a pen. For the next 20 minutes, let's explore both sides of the proverbial coin in our lives, and talk Duality with Archangel Cassiel!*

*Close your eyes and be still. Pay attention to how the air feels as it passes through your nostrils. Notice the natural rhythm your breath takes. In and out. In and out. In and out. Feel the difference between your inhales and your exhales. What happens physically on an inhalation? And an exhalation? What happens emotionally? Mentally? Notice the upbeats and downbeats of your rhythmic breathing. How do they differ? Now imagine you have an invisible line down the middle of your body, dividing you into right and left hemispheres. Breathe fully into the right side of your body. Take notice of any sensations, visions, thoughts or phrases that arise. Now breathe into the left side and pay attention to anything that arises there. Are there any differences between your two halves? Now breathe into both halves simultaneously, rejoining your body. Call in Cassiel and ask him to help you embrace the gift of duality in your life by sharing his gifts in a tangible, verifiable way now. Pay attention to how he comes through for you – do you see, hear or feel him? Does your intuition kick in or do you just know the answers? Or are you using your imagination to complete the experiment? When you are ready, open your eyes.*

*Take your journal and write down a list of 5 positive and 5 negative experiences you've had in your life.*

*Now grab your lists and the coin.*

*For this experiment: Heads = Positive*
*Tails = Negative*

*Start with your positive list. Take the first experience and flip the coin.*

*If it is Heads, close your eyes and tune in. Explore the positive aspects of the experience. What good came out of it? What did you learn? What is the overall feeling of the event?*

*If it is Tails, close your eyes and tune in. Explore the negative aspects of the experience. Deconstruct the moment and see it from a different perspective.*

*Or deconstruct it and imagine making the opposite choice.*

*How does the outcome change? What good came out of it? What do you learn? What is the overall feeling of the event?*

*Write your messages in your journal.*

*Rinse, lather, and repeat until you have completed all 5 events on both lists, 10 total.*

*Upon completion, reflect on your messages and record your observations in your journal. How does seeing both sides of your experiences affect your understanding of duality? Did you receive any surprising insights? How did Archangel Cassiel come through for you? What did he have to share? Take time now to express your gratitude to Cassiel for his loving perspective!*

## *Experiment**

*Grab your yoga mat, pillow, blanket (if desired), voice recording device, journal and a pen. For the next 40 minutes, follow Archangel Cassiel on a journey through one of your previous incarnations in a Past Life Regression.*

*Find a quiet space where you will not be disturbed. Roll out your yoga mat, lay down on your back, arms relaxed at your sides, legs loose with your feet falling naturally out to their outer sides. Start your voice recorder. When you are asked a question, speak your answers out loud, so the voice recorder can catch it for you. You will want to review it after the experiment. Close your eyes gently. Call in Cassiel and ask him share his reincarnation wisdom with you through a past (or future) life regression that is relevant to your current life growth, in a tangible, verifiable way now. Notice how he comes through for you. Do you see, hear or feel his presence? Does he reveal himself in your regression?*

*Feel all the places where your body contacts the mat, supporting you fully to the earth. You feel secure, safe to begin this journey.*

*Notice your eyes, how your upper lids make contact with your lower lids. You are relaxed and turn your attention inward. Focus on your internal breath.*

*Your eyes are so relaxed; they feel as though they want to remain closed on their own.*

*If you test them, they want to remain closed, and almost won't open.*

*This feels so relaxing; you allow it to spread from your eyelids into every part of your body. And the relaxation spreads into your mind. And it now moves to your soul.*

*Let any sound you hear around you simply take you deeper into relaxation.*
*Any sound, any disruption, even your own breathing, or thoughts in your consciousness, just takes you deeper into relaxation. You are extremely relaxed.*

*As your eyelids remain closed and relaxed, allow that feeling to spread to your forehead. Just let the muscles loosen and relax in your forehead. It spreads to your face, back of your head, jaw, neck and shoulders, loosening all the muscles until you are soft and deeply relaxed.*

*Feel the relaxation spread even further, down through your shoulders into your arms, all the way to your fingertips. Feel the relaxation as your fingers and fingertips completely let go.*

*Now allow the relaxation you feel begin to spread down your body to your chest and upper back, mid back and your abdomen, spreading down into your pelvis, and fully into your entire lower body. You are feeling beautifully heavy and relaxed. From the top of your head all the way down to the tips of your toes, you are pleasantly relaxed and comfortable. You are in a relaxing daydream state, breathing gently.*

*Your legs relax, feeling heavy and comfortably weighted. The relaxation spreads down from the tops of your thighs, into your knees, calves, shins, ankles, and all the way into your feet, stretching out to your toes. All muscles in your legs and feet are soft and relaxed. You are comfortable, completely relaxed from head to toe, and go deeper with every new breath.*

*Now imagine that you're on a spiral staircase that leads to your inner being. Start walking down the staircase. Every stair brings you deeper and closer to your Akashic memory, your Divine consciousness. With each step you are more and more relaxed, feeling calm and comfortable.*
*Five ... You descend this stairway of relaxation, each step becoming more and more relaxed.*
*Four ... Step by step. Left foot, right foot, left foot, right foot. Your feet bring you closer, deeper, into your Divine memory.*
*Three ... You are at the half point on the stairs, walking deeper into your Divine consciousness. So very relaxed.*
*Two ... You are almost to the bottom of the stairs. Ahead, you see a gorgeous swirling portal of light. You've seen this portal before. It feels safe and familiar. You remember feeling secure inside it. It leads you to all your past and future lives, and any other places and times of significance to you. It is eternal, never ending.*

*And One ... You've reached the bottom of the stairs, deep within your Akashic memory. You are so relaxed and comfortable. You are standing at the foot of the portal. Beautiful white light beckons you to walk through and see what is offered on the other side. You feel extremely relaxed and secure. You take a step forward into the swirling light and find yourself in a new place. Standing there, what do you notice? Look down at your feet. What are you standing on? What does it look like beneath your feet?*

*Looking at your feet, what are you wearing? What is on your feet?*

*Raise your gaze to your lower body. What are you wearing on your lower body? What do you observe about your what you are wearing?*

*Raise your gaze to your upper body. What are you wearing on your upper body? What do you observe about what you are wearing?*

*Is the quality of what you are wearing higher or lower quality?*

*Is there anything distinctive on or about your clothing that indicates who you might be at this moment? Are you carrying anything?*

*Raise your gaze now to your head. What do you notice about your head and hair? Are you wearing any articles of clothing or adornments of interest?*

*Are you male or female here? How old are you at this time and place? Are you moving or still? Are you standing, sitting or lying down, at the present time?*

*Are you alone or are others with you? What is your relationship to them? How are you interacting with them?*

*Look past your body now and observe your environment. What do your eyes see? What do your ears hear? What do you feel? Are your hands touching anything? What does your nose smell? What does your tongue taste?*

*You become aware of the events and circumstances at*

*this time. What are your current circumstances? What are you currently doing? What is happening at this moment? What are your feelings and emotions right now?*

*Move a head a little in time in this life. What is happening now? What is occurring at this time? What are you doing at this time and place? What are your emotions and experiences at this time and place?*

*You move even further ahead in this life. What is happening? What are you experiencing, feeling, observing? How old are you now? What are your circumstances now? What events are occurring now?*

*Letting events proceed to their climax or conclusion, what is happening now? What are you experiencing, feeling, and observing now? What else do you notice about this time and place?*

*Now allow time to move ahead to another event later in this lifetime.*
*What do you notice now? What has happened in this lifetime to date, as you advance through the years?*

*Are you alone or with someone now? What is happening now? How old are you now?*
*What events are occurring - especially those that brought you to this event? What are you experiencing, feeling, observing?*

*Letting events proceed to their climax or conclusion, what is happening now? What are you experiencing, feeling, and observing now? What else do you notice about this time and place?*

*As you move ahead to the final moments in that lifetime,*

*what do you notice? How old are you now? Who is with you, or are you alone? What are your circumstances, and what events are occurring?*

*What is it that makes this your final moment in this lifetime? What is important to note about this particular moment? What are your emotions, feelings, and experiences at this moment?*

*Let time progress, and allow yourself to cross the threshold, stepping out of your body.*

*Look back at yourself, the body you have just left. Is it alone or are there others around you, either in spirit or in the flesh? Look ahead slightly in time. What occurs in that place following your passing?*

*Now let's move upward a little bit and turn around to see the light waiting for you.*
*Who is there to meet you now? Who else? Move toward the light, feeling the light embrace you. Feel the love of those who are in your soul group.*

*Now pause for a moment and look back at the life you are just leaving. What was the lesson or purpose for your entry into this particular lifetime? Did you learn this lesson? Accomplish this purpose?*

*Allow any healing to take place, any healing of the soul that is needed from this lifetime.*
*Let that take place now as we again move into the light. Let the embrace of the light welcome you. Move into the light and feel the presence of your Divine Source.*

*Are there any other special beings there for you? Are there any teachers, guides or other higher beings there?*

*As you join them, what do they say, do, ask?*
*Review the lessons, events and accomplishments of the lifetime you are now leaving.*
*What do you notice? What are your conclusions? What are your joys, regrets? Any other feelings?*

*And now, as this journey concludes, move once again, back through the portal that led to this lifetime. Move to the stairs that brought you here. As you return, walking back up the staircase to full conscious awareness, you find that you can take the memories of this journey, and any lessons, with you for future use, feeling clear and confident that this is helpful information.*

*You begin to walk back up the staircase.*
*One ... Every single step brings you back into conscious awareness.*
*Two ... Become aware of background noise in your environment, sensations on your skin, your face. You have deep clarity and wisdom. And a deeper awareness of the patterns and cycles connected between your lives.*
*Three ... You are half way up the staircase, feeling less dreamy, more present with every moment that passes.*
*Four ... Almost to the top of the stairs now feeling very present.*
*Five ... Your eyes open gently. You are awake and aware, feeling refreshed, alive, and enlightened.*

*Upon completion, stop your voice recorder and take time to reflect on your journey, recording your observations in your journal. How does your past life memory relate to your current life? What lessons can be applied? How did Archangel Cassiel come through for you? What did he have to share? Take time now to express your gratitude to Cassiel for his regression wisdom!*

## Feathers of Wisdom

For an Archangel rarely called upon by the masses, Cassiel sure has a lot to offer!

Enjoy traveling but have no time? Try this: Ask Cassiel to accompany you on an Astral trip in your dreams! Visit your great grannie, the Queen of England or your best friend down the street and have a blast knowing your travel companion has your back!

Feeling unsafe in your psychic realm lately? Try this: Call on Cassiel to remove all negative entities and energies from your auric field and personal environment, protecting you ever more from psychic attack. He will also help you change your reality so fear doesn't hold you back from using your gifts whenever you choose. Thanks Cassiel for being a great bouncer!

Got a head for finance? Then Cassiel is your Patron Saint! Whether it's an exchange on the stock market, a high-risk investment or a trip to Sin City, Cassiel can make sure Lady Luck is with you all the way! Try this: The next time your state jackpot is sizeable, invest the dollar and opt to choose your own numbers. Before you commit to the clerk, close your eyes, breathe deeply, and ask Cassiel to provide you with winning numbers for this current lottery, for your highest and best. Then pay attention to how Cassiel inspires you! Do you see, hear or feel your numbers for the clerk? Do you just know which ones to pick? Thanks Cassiel for the heads up! "May the odds be ev-ah in your fav-ah"! ;)

Are you an Earth sign who loves the Salt Life? Call on Cassiel to help you cleanse all negative energy using Mother Earth's oceans, lakes and rivers. Try this: After a really rough day, write out the ick on a piece of paper. Run a bath, or take a shower, bringing the paper in with you. Ask Cassiel to cleanse you of all residual ick. While you are purifying your body, rub off all the ink or lead from the paper using your fingers, and allow it to dissipate into the water and down the drain. You will feel like a new you!

Are you besties with the dolphins and the whales? Maybe you have a pet Dory? Ask Cassiel to keep your beloved sea babies safe, healthy and happy!

# Archangel Chamuel

## Angel of PEACE

Helps with:

- Love
- Peace in personal relations and world relations
- Personal purpose (career, life)
- Establishing and maintaining strong foundations
- Soul mates
- Lost items

Seasons of Love (Rent)

Five hundred twenty-five thousand
Six hundred minutes
Five hundred twenty-five thousand
Moments so dear
Five hundred twenty-five thousand
Six hundred minutes
How do you measure – measure a year?
In daylights – In sunsets
In midnights – In cups of coffee
In inches – In miles
In laughter – In strife

In - Five Hundred Twenty-Five Thousand
Six Hundred Minutes
How Do You Measure
A Year In The Life?

How About Love?
How About Love?
How About Love?
Measure In Love

Seasons of Love
Seasons of Love

Five Hundred Twenty-Five Thousand
Six Hundred Minutes
Five Hundred Twenty-Five Thousand
Journeys To Plan

Five Hundred Twenty-Five Thousand
Six Hundred Minutes
How Do You Measure The Life
Of A Woman Or A Man

In Truth That She Learned
Or In Times That He Cried
In Bridges He Burned
Or The Way That She Died

It's Time Now - To Sing Out
Though The Story Never Ends
Let's Celebrate
Remember A Year In The Life Of Friends

Remember the Love
Remember the Love
Remember the Love
Measure In Love

Oh you got to you got to remember the love,
You know that love is a gift from up above
Share love, give love, spread love
Measure, measure your life in love

Seasons Of Love
Seasons Of Love

Measure your life, measure your life in love

The lyrics to this song from the musical Rent speak for themselves. Whatever your question, love is the answer. Let's allow Archangel Chamuel to introduce us to this healing force for our individual needs and for the greater good.

## Intentions*

Sit comfortably, with your spine straight, feet flat to the floor, palms turned up in your lap. Close your eyes and connect with your breath. Inhale through your nose to the count of 3, and exhale out of your mouth to the count of 5. Repeat this breathing rhythm 5 more times, allowing your breath to expand your abdomen and lungs a little more each time. Inhale, and exhale. Inhale, and exhale. Inhale, and exhale. Inhale, and exhale. Inhale, and exhale. Imagine you are sitting on a large jut of rock at the top of a mountain. You feel very heavy. Your body is fully connected to this rock. You and the rock are one. The pink sunset is warm on your face, shining on your skin as you look up into the sky. Surrounded in this colourful glow, you feel peaceful and secure with your place on Mother Earth. Smiling softly, bring your attention to your ever-beating heart. Spread your chest wide, allowing the sunset energy to fill it fully. As you enjoy this energy boost, a figure appears at your side. It is Archangel Chamuel. Repeat this intention out loud: Hi Chamuel! I'm honoured to meet you! I'd love to learn about your gifts, and how you communicate with me. I'm ready to receive your guidance. Please open my heart fully and show me how to achieve peace in my life through love, in a tangible, verifiable way now. I'm so grateful you have made it so!

If you wish, take this time now to add a personal intention for this experiment.

Chamuel joins you in soaking up the sunset energy, enhancing your energy field. You now have a strongly established foundation from which to begin. You feel fully connected and ready to have this adventure. Gently open your eyes.

## *Experiment*

*Grab your journal and a pen. For the next 20 minutes, allow Archangel Chamuel to write, or jazz up, your personal purpose and life mission! He loves to infuse lives with love!*

*Find a quiet, comfortable place to sit, close your eyes and connect to your breath. Give your breath the colour pink. Visualize this pink air travelling in through your nose, filling your mouth and throat. With each fresh inhale, it expands into your chest area, filling your lungs and heart space, upper and lower back, abdomen and pelvis. Your entire core is glowing with the pink essence of Chamuel. Invite him to guide you to your Life Purpose and Mission. Ask him to help you have an open heart and willing soul as you receive tangible, verifiable answers now. Notice how Chamuel comes through for you – do you see, hear or feel him? Does an unseen force guide your hand? Are you using your imagination to complete the work? When you are ready, gently open your eyes.*

*Now grab your journal and finish the following statements by tuning into your heart space. Close your eyes and breathe deeply, clearing your mind and focusing on your heart before each statement. Don't overthink your answers! Go with your first thought, image or memory.*

*1/ My heart dances and my soul sings when I…*
*2/ I giggle and smile when I…*
*3/ When I was a kid, my favourite activities to participate in were…*

*4/ When I was a teen, my favourite activities to participate in were…*
*5/ As an adult, my favourite activities to participate in are…*
*6/ I feel most alive when I am…*
*7/ I am truly proud of myself when I…*
*8/ My role model(s) in life is… I admire them most because they…*
*9/ I am a natural at...*
*10/ I am often asked for help with…*
*11/ If I were a professor, I would love to teach…*
*12/ I deeply value… (choose 3-5 words)*
*13/ If today is my last day to live, I regret …*
*14/ I stand up and add my voice for the cause(s) of…*
*15/ I'd like to combine my skills, abilities, beliefs and passions to serve others by…*

*Now review your answers and use them to create your unique Life Purpose Affirmation, with the below statements. Again, close your eyes, breathe and connect to your heart space before completing each sentence.*

*1/ I want to do/be/have…*
*2/ I want to help… (who)*
*3/ My actions result in…*
*4/ I generate value/worth by/through…*

*Now clarify your statement using the below statement, or by creating your own:*

*I ______. I help ______ by ______ with/through my ______.*

*Once you have your Life Purpose Affirmation, repeat the statement out loud 3 times. The first time, speak through your solar plexus. The second time, speak through your throat. The third time, speak through your heart. Notice any differences in the delivery of your affirmation. How do you feel speaking it out loud? Does it resonate with you or need some tweaking? If the latter, take time now to adjust your affirmation until it rings true in your core. Does it inspire you to follow through?*

*Upon completion, take a moment to reflect on your insights and record your experience in your journal. Did you learn something new about yourself and your purpose? Did you feel a shift in your direction? How does this affirmation help you moving forward? How did Archangel Chamuel show up for you? What did he have to share? Take time now to express gratitude to Chamuel for his loving direction!*

## *Experiment*

*Grab a pair of inexpensive glasses, pink coloured cellophane, crafting kit, journal and a pen. For the next 30 minutes, let's explore conflict resolution Chamuel-style!*

*The old adage: "…seeing the world through rose-coloured glasses" is often used in a negative connotation. It implies that the individual in question is not seeing reality, or not recognizing the truth as it is, choosing a more pleasant, fantasy-like perspective to believe. Yet who's to say that is necessarily a bad thing? In this experiment, let's switch things up, and use our own pair of rose-coloured glasses to see personal conflict through the eyes of love and find peace!*

*Find a flat surface to lay out your crafting kit, pink cellophane, glasses, journal and pen. Sit quietly for a moment, close your eyes, and bring your attention to your heart space. Call in Chamuel and ask him to fill your heart with love, compassion and clarity and guide your hands to infuse everything you create with his wisdom, in a tangible, verifiable way now. Then take the pink cellophane and cut out lens-sized shapes you can adhere to your glasses. You can get as creative as you'd like – go 60's cat style, make triangles, circles or squares, whatever you desire! Attach them over the existing lenses with glue or double-sided tape to the frame. If you wish, continue decorating the frames with jewels, beads, stickers, ribbons, feathers or paint. When your rose-coloured glasses are complete, set them aside for the next step.*

*Sit down with your journal. Think of a personal conflict you are currently having with another person (or had in the past that was never resolved) and write down the circumstances as you see it. What started the conflict? Why are you hurt, angry, upset, sad, frustrated, or any other feeling that comes up, when you think about this person and/or the issue? What do you feel is the core of the matter? What would you like the other person to change in order to resolve this conflict? What do you need to feel resolved?*

*Now write about the same conflict from the other person's perspective. Be an observer. What started the conflict? Why are they hurt, angry, upset, sad, frustrated, or any other feeling that comes up, when they think about you and/or this issue? What do they feel is the core of the matter? What would they like you to change in order to resolve this conflict? What do they need to feel resolved?*

*Now grab your Chamuel infused rose-coloured glasses and put them on! Re-read both accounts of the conflict and write a peaceful solution, seeing the situation through your heart. Notice how Chamuel comes through for you – do you see, hear or feel him? Does an unseen force guide your hand? Are you using your imagination to complete the work?*

*Take a few minutes to reflect on the experience and record your observations in your journal. What did Chamuel have to share with you about your conflict? Do you notice any shifts in your perspective? Are you more at peace with your situation? How did he show up for you? Take time now to express gratitude to Chamuel for his loving wisdom!*

## Feathers of Wisdom

Want a little love pick-me-up – a reminder that you **are** LOVE no matter where you are? Archangel Chamuel says try this: Put a small to medium polished Rose Quartz crystal inside your bra or shirt pocket, close to your heart! Or wear a rose quartz pendant, earrings or a bracelet on your left arm. If you'd like to carry around more than one crystal, keep a small velvet pouch in your pocket, or purchase worry stones. Rose Quartz is well known for its gentle heart healing and unconditional love. If you want to ensure you are always coming from your heart space, this is an effective way to make it happen!

Having relationship issues and need guidance? Try this: Purchase a rose coloured glass or buy a wine goblet from the dollar store and partially fill it with pink marbles or stones. Keep a small notepad or post-its and a pen close by. Whenever you need to, write your issue and your desired outcome on a piece of paper, fold it and place it in the glass. Ask Chamuel to handle it for you, for your highest and best. Thank him for making it so, then release the issue from your control, trusting that love will prevail! When the issue is resolved, burn, bury or rinse the papers to release and transmute the energy with gratitude!

Missing an earring? Can't find your phone? Chamuel is an amazing detector of lost things! Try this: The next time an object goes missing, call on Chamuel to help you find it. Say: Chamuel, thank you for helping me find my missing _____ in a tangible, verifiable way now. I'm grateful it is back where it needs to be, happy, healthy and whole! Thanks for making it so! Then pay attention to any gut feelings or messages on where to look! If it is meant to be with you, it will be returned with an added infusion of love!

# Archangel Gabriel

Helps with:

- Communication & Creativity
- Integrity and truthfulness
- Mercy
- Achieving peace
- Bringing information on upcoming events, change
- New projects, jobs, moves, etc.
- Eliminating clutter

Inspiration comes in many forms and guises. Contrary to popular belief, painters, sculptors, writers & interior decorators do not hold the monopoly on what defines creative expression. The Manager who expertly diffuses a growing confrontation between two departments by offering an "outside-the-box" 3rd option; the custodian who resourcefully modifies his mop and cleaning solution with items on hand to more efficiently complete his task; the severely arthritic man who creates an invaluable tool to help him put his socks on in the morning using cardboard, shoestring and a couple of hooks – these are all practical examples of creative inspiration!

And there is great value in channeling your inner kindergartener and playing with paint, clay, colour, fabric, etc. An invigorating, satisfying, and often healing, process occurs when you reconnect with that urge to create for creation's sake. You "plug in" to your true nature, and unlock possibilities you may not have thought up otherwise.

This creativity is also a necessity when dealing with your fellow humans. The secret to successful communication, believe it or not, is speaking truthfully from your heart-centered space. Sometimes this requires a little bit of creative finesse to make sure your words and their intended meaning are received in a way conducive to mutual understanding, respect & harmony. This includes those conversations you hold with yourself as well!

## *Intentions**

Close your eyes and connect to your breath. Give your breath a colour. Go with the first one you see, hear, feel, or sense. As you inhale deeply, visualize your coloured breath filtering throughout your body. Bring your breath to your feet, ankles, calves and shins. Breathe into your knees, thighs, pelvic area and navel. Notice how your coloured breath takes on a shimmer as you fill your abdomen, lungs and chest. This shimmer triggers a warm tingling vibration as it enters your heart and into your throat area. It swirls and expands your throat space, making room for free and limitless expression. This feeling carries up your neck and into your face, pausing to expand at your third eye and crown. As you enjoy this limitlessness, you are surrounded in a white misty cloud of vapor. You take your hands and touch this cloud, swirling it in front of you. As you do, you feel something, and part the mist to reveal it. Archangel Gabriel appears. She is happy you have initiated this meeting! You connect your heart to hers, and repeat this intention out loud: Hi Gabriel! It's an honour to meet you! I want to get to know you better. I'd love to learn about your gifts, and how you communicate with me. I'm ready to receive your guidance. Please show me inspiration in areas of my life that can benefit, in a tangible, verifiable way now. I'm so grateful you have made it so!

If you wish, take this time now to add a personal intention for this experiment.

Gabriel gently touches one hand to your throat and another to your forehead. You see a brilliant flash of light and feel you are a completely open vessel to receive her wisdom. Gently open your eyes.

## Experiment

*Grab your coloured pencils or markers, blank mandala**, clipboard, journal and a pen. For the next 30 minutes, let's embrace your inner kindergartener and get creative with Archangel Gabriel!*

*Find a comfortable place to sit. Close your eyes and connect to your breath. Call in Archangel Gabriel and allow her to turn your mind off. Ask her to show you how to access her wisdom through your creative hands and heart, in a tangible, verifiable way now. "Be" in silence. Relish the peace and solitude that silence brings. If thoughts get in the way, focus on your breath. When you are ready, gently open your eyes.*

*Take your mandala and your colour tools of choice and get comfortable. Maintain the silence you've discovered, allow Gabriel to influence your colour & design choices, and get lost in the blissful flow of creation! Be aware of any insights, inspirations, interesting thoughts or moments of clarity that arise during this time. What is the message in the mandala? Does Gabriel speak to you or show you? Is your hand perhaps guided by an unseen energy? If thoughts do pop in, are they random and clarifying?*

*Upon completion, take a few minutes to reflect on your mandala and record your experience in your journal. How did Archangel Gabriel show up for you? What did she have to share? Take time now to express gratitude to Gabriel for her wisdom!*

***If you wish, I've provided a blank mandala at the end of this chapter. Feel free to make a copy & use it for this experiment.*

## Experiment*

*Grab your yoga mat, pillow, blanket (if desired), journal and a pen. For the next 20 minutes, allow Gabriel to offer guidance on how to communicate successfully with your loved ones!*

*Find a quiet space to roll out your yoga mat and get comfortable. Sit cross-legged with your spine straight or lie down, whichever you prefer. Relax your legs and arms, close your eyes and breathe deeply. Take a moment to think of a relationship with a loved one that you'd like to make better. Perhaps you just don't see "eye to eye", or you don't understand one another. Maybe every time you talk, it ends in an argument. Or maybe you have an issue between the two of you that feels like you'll never get past. When you've chosen a person, ask Gabriel to come in and facilitate healthier communication between the two of you. Ask her to show you the other person from a higher, more loving perspective in a tangible, verifiable way now. Notice how Gabriel shows up for you. Do you see, hear or feel her? Do you sense her presence, or just know she's there?*

*Now breathe deeply with your diaphragm. Allow your belly to rise and fall, like you are a baby sleeping in a crib. You are feeling relaxed and calm. Now picture your loved one clearly in your mind. Remember, if you can, the first memory you have with this individual. What happened during the memory? How did you feel about them? Now think about the current issue you have with them. How did it start? What happened? What do you see as being the heart of the matter? How do you feel about this person right now? How do you feel about this issue? What do you wish would happen between the two of you? Do you desire resolution or change? Connect directly with those feelings now.*

*When you are ready, bring your attention to your heart chakra. Imagine swirls and sparkles of pink light dancing around and through your heart, expanding its energy field out 30 feet from your body in every direction. Bring your attention to the space about 4 inches above your heart. This is your high heart. Imagine swirls and sparkles of pale pink mixed with an azure blue moving through this area, expanding its energy field out 30 feet from your body in every direction. And bring your attention to your throat chakra. Imagine this chakra lit up in a beautiful rich blue light, dancing out 30 feet from your body in every direction. Now expand your third eye and crown chakras together, visualizing a wonderful blend of indigo and translucent white light reaching out 30 feet from your body in every direction. Allow all these high frequency energies to mingle and meld tenderly, creating an incredible symphony of light and sound throughout your physical and auric fields.*

*Your body hums with these new vibrational combinations, and you feel pleasantly light, floating effortlessly out of your body. A single cord of light remains connected to your high heart as you expand into this energy. This is the energy field where your highest self aspect exists. You are your highest self now, feeling detached from the density of your human form. From this vibrational frequency, you see this world differently. You see this life with the eyes and knowledge of an angel.*

*As your high self, you are inspired to seek out your loved one in human form. You find them sleeping peacefully in their bed. As your high self, you have the ability to enter their dreams. You invite them to join you, so you can explore this dimension together. They agree and you two glide together through the energy, frolicking through these universal fields. You realize this is a wonderful time to discuss your human relationship while you are both viewing each other with your divine eyes open. Ask your loved one now for permission to talk. If they agree, take this time now to have a conversation. (If they do not, explore these questions on your own.)*

*What is the heart of the matter from their perspective? What are they here to learn and work on? What part do you play in that goal?*

*What is the heart of the matter for you? What are you here to learn and work on? What part do they play in your goal?*

*Together, look over your current lives and review the bigger picture, the highest spiritual vision you can access. What do you see for yourself? For your loved one? For both of you together?*

*Ask them how you can best communicate with them so both of you can feel heard and understood? How can you support one another moving forward?*

*Is there an opportunity to offer or receive mercy? What does that look and feel like? Is there anything else you or your loved one wish to share with one another?*

*With this high wisdom revealed, you both agree to honour each other with honesty and integrity upon your return. Take time now to allow your energies to meld, acknowledging the love and oneness divinity you both share, and feel energized to continue your human experience together.*

*It is time for you both to return. You send them back into their dreams, and pour yourself back into your physical body, retaining the Divine wisdom and loving energy exchange you've both shared. Become aware of your breathing and wiggle your fingers and toes. When you are ready, gently open your eyes, feeling relaxed, peaceful and confident in your guidance!*

*Upon completion, take a moment to reflect on your experience and record your observations in your journal. Did you receive any unexpected insights? Were you able to see or feel peace? How did Archangel Gabriel come through for you? What did she have to share? Take time now to express gratitude to Gabriel for her presence on this journey!*

## Feathers of Wisdom

Feeling stuck? Ask for Gabriel's De-cluttering Service!

Just like the intention setting meditation at the start of this experiment, it is important to always create space for new inspiration to come in. Clutter can be physical, mental and emotional – stuff that no longer serves you - leaving blocks in the direct flow of your goal.

When you are feeling frustrated, unable to start or complete a project, or move forward on an issue (career, personal or other), ask Gabriel for some instant de-cluttering! Then take a break - go for a walk outside, or switch tasks – do something different for 10 minutes to an hour. Make sure to breathe and clear your head during that time. Exhale the frustration out, completely emptying your lungs. As you inhale, feel Gabriel's loving assistance expand your body, making room for a fresh perspective.

When it feels right to do so, shift the focus from your body to your mind. Imagine that with every inhale, sage smoke is entering your third eye, into your brain, gently dissipating all negative thoughts, beliefs, and blocks, clearing space for the next working "aha" moment. Exhale fully. Repeat this pattern until you feel clear.

When you are ready, ask Gabriel to fill the spaces you just made with inspiring solutions to your issues, and then return to the task at hand! She'll make you feel like a magician pulling a rabbit out of your hat! ;)

Thanks Gab for the rabbits and the spring clean!

Having trouble getting your needs met with your lover? Try this: Call on Gabriel to oversee your conflict and help both sides to open their hearts to one another. Then, instead of telling your partner what you want them to do, give them what *you* desire! For example, you wish your lover would be more romantic with you. So leave a love note on his car windshield or in his lunch. Or you love when your partner takes care of odd jobs around the house, or does favours, for you. So surprise them by taking their car and filling up their tank. You love hearing how attractive you look in your clothes. So compliment them on how great they look or smell on their way to work. We teach others how we wish to be treated. So help your partner out and see where it leads! Gabriel enjoys happy, healthy humans communicating through love and is happy to be of service!

Stacey Brown

# Archangel Haniel

## Angel of INTUITION

Helps with:

- Empathic & intuitive abilities
- Accessing your gifts & talents
- Emotion
- Finding grace
- Making friends

One of the constants in our human existence is the Moon. While the Sun's masculine illumination exposes our truth in a very bold, very physical way, the feminine Moon illuminates that truth with the softer, gentler light of intuition and inner wisdom. Much is being written about the Divine Feminine taking center stage today to end an unhealthy patriarchal paradigm and bring back emotional balance. For too long, we have been flowing without an ebb, our natural tides of balance and harmony blocked by fear and abuse of power. Intuition has been beaten and tortured out of us, scoffed at and deemed as "snake oil", devil's work, voodoo, or silly nonsense. Yet we need both our masculine and feminine sides to integrate for us to be whole, to live our truth fully with grace and gratitude. We *need* to trust our inner guidance now more than ever before to steer us back on course to the only destination that truly exists – love.

I recently attended a seminar by Sage Melillo that discussed the difference between emotions and feelings. There are only 2 emotions: Love and Fear (Marianne Williamson speaks of this often). If you are not in Love, then you are in Fear. Feelings are the "states of mind" your ego creates to keep you feeling victimized, trapped or hooked in and by the physical world. The ego is terrified of 2 things: being annihilated and losing something. Each feeling (state of mind) falls into one of those choices. When we dissolve the states of mind keeping us stuck in unhealthy or outdated patterns and cycles, we free ourselves to "be", to follow our inner guidance, access our gifts, talents and truly embrace joy without all our illusory baggage. We become fully integrated beings. Archangel Haniel, the Angel of the Moon, enjoys nothing more than to show us how to ebb and flow ourselves into the bliss we already are.

## Intentions*

Close you eyes and connect with your breath. Inhale deeply, and exhale. Breathe deeply and slowly. Inhale, and exhale. Breathe in peace, and breathe out that which no longer serves you. Visualize yourself lying on a raft at the shore of the ocean. You float effortlessly, moving with the ebb and flow of the ocean. Inhale and exhale as though your breath is joined to the tide. Breathe in the salty air and allow your soul to be cleansed.

It is midnight and the moonlight cascades delicately over your body and onto the water. You stare at its majesty, high above the earth's atmosphere, imagining what the view is like in reverse. As you contemplate this experience, the moonlight grows brighter all around you and the sound of the ocean softens and fades. The moon moves toward you on the raft, growing larger. As it gets within reaching distance, it is transformed into a gorgeous pink and gold orb. You realize you are in Archangel Haniel's presence! You reach out to connect with her energy. Repeat out loud this intention: Hi Haniel! I'm honoured to meet you! Please introduce me to your purpose! I am an open vessel, ready to receive your all-encompassing wisdom and am so grateful for your intuitive energy! Please show me the depth of my own power, my own light, in a tangible, verifiable way now. Thank you for making it so!

If you wish, take this time now to add a personal intention for this experiment.

Haniel's energy travels through your body, preparing you for the journey ahead. When you are ready, gently open your eyes.

## *Experiment**

*Grab your yoga mat, journal and a pen. For the next 20 minutes, let Haniel help you dissolve states of mind that no longer serve you, and enter your bliss!*

*Find a quiet space to lay out your yoga mat. Sit or lie down and get comfortable. Close your eyes and connect with your breath. Inhale deeply, connecting with your diaphragm, exhale fully, releasing all breath until your lungs feel completely empty. Repeat this for a moment. Call in Haniel and ask her to introduce you to your feelings, states of mind, that are perhaps holding you back or no longer serving your current path. Allow her to demonstrate her healing guidance through clarity and dissolution, in a tangible, verifiable way now. Allow your breath to find its natural rhythm.*

*Imagine yourself standing at the edge of a large, dimly lit room. As you look around, the room appears empty. You are alone. Out of the corner of your eye, you catch movement from one of the corners. A tiny light appears, small at first, then it grows wider. You feel a friendly, loving presence emanating from that light. The ceiling begins to take on an iridescent glow. As the light presence expands into the room, it reflects off the ceiling, revealing what is providing such colour. Beautiful bubbles of all colours and sizes are filling the room. The presence speaks to you. It is Haniel. She offers these bubbles as a gift, a tool for revealing what can be dissipated, and make room for joy in every moment. If you choose to explore her offer, she will show you how, and support you every step of the way.*

*Curious, you accept her gift, eager for her instruction. She tells you that the room you are in represents your mind, and each bubble represents a feeling, a state of mind, that keeps you from living within your true joy. Walk around the room and examine all the bubbles. As you do, you notice that each bubble has a dominant feeling associated with it. Choose three bubbles – either the first three you see or the first three that resonate with you. Carefully take them in your hands and bring them into the center of the room. Haniel has prepared a sparkling chair, made of angelic light, and invites you to sit. On the left is a small tray for you to place your bubbles. With your hands free, you sit in the chair. What does it feel like? What happens while you are there?*

*Haniel guides you to pick up the first bubble. Examine its shape, size and colour. Does it have a predominant colour? If so, what chakra is it connected to? What feeling is associated with this sphere? What do you need to understand about it? How does it impact your life, your goals? Think of the very first time you felt this feeling. What memory is attached to it? What happened? Who was there? What was the outcome of the situation? What was the core of the matter for you?*

*Now Haniel asks you to continue to hold the bubble and hang onto that memory and the feeling(s) that came up. Sit in this feeling and stay with it. Feel it deeply. If your mind wanders to a different memory or a different thought altogether, gently bring yourself back to the bubble you are holding. Sit inside this feeling, this state of mind, and notice what comes up for you. Maybe you feel it intensely for a while and the feeling lightens up. Or a release happens through tears. Or you hang on so long it becomes laughter. As you are present for this experience, the bubble in your hands begins to grow and expand in size. It softly envelops your entire body, leaving you pleasantly warm and safe. When you can no longer hold the feeling, or the feeling has shifted inside you, the bubble dissolves, leaving its luminescent colours all over you. You are forever covered in an angelic reminder of your true loving essence and the integration of that which no longer serves into that which does.*

*When you are ready, repeat the process with your second bubble. Is there anything different about the shape, size and colour of this one? Does it have a predominant colour? If so, what chakra is it connected to? What feeling is associated with this sphere? What do you need to understand about it? How does it impact your life, your goals? Think of the very first time you felt this feeling. What memory is attached to it? What happened? Who was there? What was the outcome of the situation? What was the core of the matter for you?*

*Continue to hold the bubble and hang onto that memory and the feeling(s) that came up. Sit in this feeling and stay with it. Feel it deeply. If your mind wanders to a different memory or a different thought altogether, gently bring yourself back to the bubble you are holding. Sit inside this feeling, this state of mind, and notice what comes up for you.*

*Fully present, you see the bubble in your hands begin to grow and expand in size. It softly envelops your entire body, leaving you pleasantly warm and safe. When you can no longer hold the feeling, or the feeling has shifted inside you, the bubble dissolves, leaving its luminescent colours all over you. You are forever covered in an angelic reminder of your true loving essence and the integration of that which no longer serves into that which does.*

*When you are ready, repeat the process with your third bubble. Is there anything different about the shape, size and colour of this one? Does it have a predominant colour? If so, what chakra is it connected to? What feeling is associated with this sphere? What do you need to understand about it? How does it impact your life, your goals? Think of the very first time you felt this feeling. What memory is attached to it? What happened? Who was there? What was the outcome of the situation? What was the core of the matter for you?*

*Hold the bubble and hang onto that memory and the feeling(s) that came up. Sit in this feeling and stay with it. Feel it deeply. If your mind wanders to a different memory or a different thought altogether, gently bring yourself back to the bubble you are holding. Sit inside this feeling, this state of mind, and notice what comes up for you.*

*Once again, the bubble in your hands begins to grow and expand in size. It softly envelops your entire body, leaving you pleasantly warm and safe. When you can no longer hold the feeling, or the feeling has shifted inside you, the bubble dissolves, leaving its luminescent colours all over you. You are forever covered in an angelic reminder of your true loving essence and the integration of that which no longer serves into that which does.*

*As the third feeling, state of mind, is released, the room around you changes. You are now sitting on a park bench next to Haniel in an outdoor park by a calm, still lake. It is a warm, breezy spring day and carefree children are playing by the water blowing beautiful bubbles into the air. You are free! Haniel invites you to rise from the bench, floating with the joy from within! She reaches out and gives you a loving hug, embracing you in her wings of friendship. Hand in hand, you walk along the water, enjoying each other's company, integrating this new energy now!*

*When you are ready, bring your attention to your breath. Wiggle your fingers and toes and come back into the room. Slowly open your eyes.*

*Take a moment to reflect on your insights and record your experience in your journal. How did Archangel Haniel show up for you? What did she have to share? Do you feel any different after dissolving unneeded states of mind? Take time now to express gratitude to Haniel for her wisdom!*

## Experiment

*Grab your yoga mat, pillow, blanket, instrumental crystal bowl music, journal, pen, water and a timer (if desired). For the next hour you will be exploring the depths of your intuitive and empathic abilities with the gentle guidance of Archangel Haniel through a Stillpoint breath work meditation.*

*Start your music and lay out your yoga mat in a quiet space. Place your journal, pen, running timer (set for 1 hour) and water close by so you can access it as soon as the meditation is complete. Make sure you get very comfortable, as you will be laying in the same position for the entire experiment. Adjust your pillow and blanket. Call in Haniel and ask her to bring you deep into your intuitive layers, allowing you to expand beyond any limits you have knowingly or unknowingly set for yourself, in a tangible, verifiable way now. Notice how she comes through for you. Do you experience her with your 5 senses and/or your 6th sense? Does she offer insight into current personal situations or past incidents? Are you able to go deeper into your abilities than before?*

*When you are ready, close your eyes and begin to breath in and out of your mouth as though you are panting. Aim to have the rhythm of your panting match two inhale/exhale cycles per 1 second. You will be breathing through your partially opened mouth for the entire meditation. Your mouth will get dry, and about 10 minutes after you've begun, you may even feel like you are hyperventilating. Don't panic. This is normal. Do your best to swallow as little as possible and relax into the rhythm of your breath. Continue this for the duration of the experiment and notice what you notice. Some people have experienced a stopping of the breath for a short duration of time (around the 35-40 minute mark). If this happens to you, stay calm and ride the wave. This means you've reached Stillpoint! There is no danger to you. Your body will naturally breath again as needed. In the meantime, embrace this moment of Stillpoint and communicate with Haniel. Get to know her and how she can help you!*

*When you come to a stopping point, either naturally or through the timer notification, begin breathing normally, closing your mouth. Swallow as needed. If you wish, you can shake out your extremities and come back into the room. When you are ready, sit up slowly, and have a drink of water.*

*Take a moment to reflect on your insights and record your experience in your journal. How did Archangel Haniel show up for you? What did she have to share? Were you able to stay present during the breath work? Did she offer any new modalities to communicate with you or simply deepen what you already work with? Take time now to express gratitude to Haniel for her wisdom!*

## Experiment

*Grab a clipboard (or go to a flat surface), 3 blank pieces of paper, a writing utensil, some meditative music and your journal. For the next 20 minutes, you will be exploring the many intuitive messages of Haniel through patterns and cycles, in a tangible, verifiable way now. Get comfortable in your space and turn on the tunes!*

*Take a moment to think about what responsibilities and events you have ahead in the next month. Are there any commitments that give you pause – not wanting to participate, not enjoying the task, etc.? Are there any you really look forward to?*

*Now choose a shape. It can be a triangle, square, circle, rectangle or star.*

*Once you have chosen, place your writing utensil to a blank sheet and close your eyes. Reconnect with Haniel's energy. Ask her to open your intuitive pathways and reveal her mysteries through all patterns and cycles occurring in your life. Notice how she comes through for you – do you see, hear or feel her presence? Do you suddenly receive insight or "just know" about your query? Does an unseen force guide your hand? Or are you using your imagination to connect?*

*When you are ready, open your eyes and begin to draw your chosen shape repeatedly. You can change the size of the shape but stick only to the one shape. Get lost in the music and repetitive flow. Contemplate your month ahead. Do you receive any insight or intuitive sense on what's to come? Any changes you wish to make?*

*When your page is full, swap it for a blank page and choose a different shape. Think about a situation in your personal life that keeps repeating. This can be attracting love interests with similar traits, continually trusting untrustworthy friends, circumstances surrounding unsuccessful financial choices, or any unwanted pattern that holds you back. Ask Haniel to give you clarity and insight on what you need to see regarding your patterns and how to break free of them. When you are ready, begin to draw your chosen shape repeatedly. You can change the size of the shape but stick only to the one shape. Get lost in the music and repetitive flow.*

*When the second page is full, swap it for a blank page and choose a different shape. When you are ready, begin to draw your chosen shape repeatedly. You can change the size of the shape but stick only to the one shape. Get lost in the music and repetitive flow. When you are finished, look at your completed page and ask Haniel to reveal a personal Divine message through the pattern.*

*Upon completion, take a moment to reflect on your insights and record your experience in your journal. How did Archangel Haniel show up for you? What did she have to share? Take time now to express gratitude to Haniel for her wisdom!*

## Feathers of Wisdom

Feeling lonely or sorry for yourself? Call on Archangel Haniel – she's your BFF forever! One of the quickest ways to receive her grace is through Gratitude!!

*Try this*: The next time you are having trouble seeing a silver lining in your cloudy day, make a list of everything you are grateful for. Could be your family, job, hobbies, or friends. If it's a particularly bleak day, start with the breath in your lungs, two sturdy legs to walk toward your goals with, clothes to keep you warm and protected, and go from there. Within a very short time, you will have a list the size of Canada, and feel more alive and energized to choose happiness in that moment! Thanks Haniel for keepin' it real!

Have trouble knowing if what you feel really belongs to you sometimes? Haniel to the rescue!

*Try this*: Go to a public place where at least 5 people are. Ask Haniel to join you. Sit quietly as an observer, and choose a random person. Ask permission from that person's high self to tap into their current emotional state, only for a moment, to explore your empathic nature. Then ask Haniel to share their emotional state with you using your given modes of receiving. Pay attention to any subtle or obvious changes in your mood, physical health; or visions and symbols you may experience. When you are finished, send love and gratitude to the person for their help in your exploration, and ask Haniel to remove all that is not yours from your auric and physical fields. When you feel like yourself again, you can repeat the experiment as many times as you wish, provided you get permission! Thanks Haniel for letting me know what's mine!

Want to stretch your superpower legs? Haniel makes a great coach!

*Try this*: The next time you and a willing friend are looking for something to do, pull some dried beans or uncooked rice from the kitchen pantry. Have them grab a handful and dump it on the table. Then, using your intuitive superpower, tell them what you see, hear, feel, smell and taste! Let your intuition and imagination go wild! Make it fun! When you have shared your insights, ask for feedback. If nothing else, you will both have created an experience to remember!

# Archangel Jeremiel

## Angel of FORGIVENESS

Helps with:

- Forgiveness: moving forward fearlessly, while in your own power
- Giving prophetic visions
- Life reviews (clarity on where we are now)
- Psychic dreams

Have you ever done a life review? 12 Step programs call this a "Step 4: Taking Personal Inventory". Many self help giants offer workshops designed to get you reflecting on past actions and behaviors to initiate change. Maybe you've participated in conventional talk therapy where a counselor asked probing questions of you to access your subconscious and bring awareness to the surface. Perhaps you've had hypnotherapy to trigger latent memories and get to the root of an issue. These are all forms of a Life Review – an opportunity to examine where you've been, learn what worked (and what didn't), and use that information to choose your present direction.

Very often, when going through a Life Review, many occasions to feel regret come to light. Consider the phrase: "We are all teachers and we are all students." In this dynamic, we are all in positions at times where we can hurt, or be hurt by, another unintentionally, or otherwise. In hindsight, we see that there was another option or choice, another path to take, that we weren't aware of, or chose not to pursue. Rather than focusing on what cannot be changed, look at what was learned from that choice, and apply that discovery to your next opportunity. We have difficulty in forgiving others we perceive have done us wrong. Why? We often cannot forgive ourselves for doing perceived wrongs to others, or to ourselves. We are the key! Forgiveness begins within. Powerful stuff…

## Intentions*

Close your eyes and breathe slowly, inhaling and exhaling deep into your core. Feel your breath filling your abdomen, gently expanding your sides, back and front like you are blowing up a beach ball or balloon. Feel the breath swirling around your internal organs. The breath finds its way into the space between your stomach and the base of your lungs. You feel an instant sensation as the breath connects and fills that area. This is your core, your true essence. Feel your core expanding now, joining up into your heart. As your core connects with this heart space, a massive orb of energy is created, enveloping your entire body, your auric layers, and out as far as you choose to project it. Sit in this love filled globe and absorb its energy! When you feel ready, invite Archangel Jeremiel to join you in this globe. He appears in front of you, sharing in your heart light. Repeat out loud this intention: Hi Jeremiel! I'm honoured to meet you! I want to get to know you better. I'd love to learn about your gifts, and how you communicate with me. I'm ready to receive your guidance. Please open my heart fully and show me the miracle of forgiveness in my life, in a tangible, verifiable way now. I'm so grateful you have made it so!

If you wish, take this time now to add a personal intention for this experiment.

Jeremiel draws closer to you, blending your energies until you are indistinguishable. You feel fully connected and ready to have this adventure. Gently open your eyes.

## Experiment

*Grab your journal and a pen. For the next 30 minutes, you will be doing a general life review.*

*In your journal, write a vertical list of the decades or phases in your life from childhood to present. (ie. Childhood, Teens, 20's, 30's, 40's etc.) Leave 3-4 lines worth of space in between each entry.*

*Choose 2-4 words that describe you in each of the decades or phases of your life - one highlighting a positive description of your experience or personal view and one highlighting a perceived negative description of your experience or personal view. If it's helpful, answer the questions: "How did I feel (about myself) back then? Who was I?" Write your words next to their corresponding decade or phase.*

*Example:*

***Childhood**:*

*Enchanting (positive)*
*Chaotic (negative)*
*Fearful (negative)*
*Don't Belong (negative)*

***20's:***

*Freedom (positive)*
*Naive (negative)*
*Lack of Confidence (negative)*
*Unsupported (negative)*

*Now ask Jeremiel to come in and help you rewrite your story using I AM statements. Take each descriptor word, one at a time. Look at it, close your eyes & breath deeply. Write down the first word or statement that comes to you, next to it. Pay attention to how Jeremiel comes through for you – do you hear, see or feel his answers? Does a word simply come to you without effort? Is your hand guided to write? Or are you using your imagination to create your statements?*

*Lather, rinse & repeat for all your descriptor words.*

*Here's what it looks like:*

***Childhood** :*

| | |
|---|---|
| *Enchanting* | *I AM Enchanting!* |
| *Chaotic* | *I AM at ease & organized.* |
| *Fearful* | *I AM Trusting! I AM Doing My Best!* |
| *Don't Belong* | *I AM Worthy! I AM Enough!* |

*When you are ready, ask Jeremiel to give you 5-10 prophetic I AM statements for the decades and phases to come. You can ask specifically for your current phase or leap into the future you! One of Jeremiel's gifts is prophetic visions... ask for yours now!*

*Upon completion, take a few minutes to reflect on your newly written story and record your experience in your journal. When you read your "I AM" statements now, how do you feel about your past? Do you notice any shifts in your emotional state? How did AA Jeremiel show up for you? What did he have to share? Take time now to express gratitude to Jeremiel for his wisdom!*

## *Experiment*

*Grab your journal and a pen. For the next 20 minutes, you will be exploring forgiveness with Archangel Jeremiel. Find a quiet spot where you will not be disturbed. Close your eyes and breathe deeply. Call in Jeremiel to guide the process. Ask him to open your heart space, help you be honest with yourself, and receive healing release for your highest and best, in a tangible, verifiable way now. When you are ready, open your eyes.*

*Now take a few minutes to write down in your journal all the perceived terrible, horrible, rotten, no good, very bad deeds you have done, things you are ashamed of, not proud of, or feel unworthy of feeling. When you've written out everything you can think of, put your journal down.*

*Close your eyes and go back into the feeling you had when you were first introduced to Jeremiel. Connect with his energy. Breathe as though you ARE Jeremiel, with a loving, forgiving heart and soul. As Jeremiel, look at yourself in your mind through his nonjudgmental, compassionate eyes. When you feel one with Jeremiel, open your eyes and read back to yourself every point you wrote in your journal, one at a time. After each one is read, Jeremiel (as you) sincerely and compassionately says: I FORGIVE YOU.*

*When the experiment is over, thank Jeremiel. Take a moment to reflect on this experience in your journal. Do you feel forgivable? Do you feel a release of any kind – physical, emotional, mental or spiritual? If you wish, write a reminder statement to yourself: I AM FORGIVEN. I FORGIVE MYSELF. I AM WORTHY. I AM LOVED. How did AA Jeremiel show up for you? What did he have to share? Take time now to express gratitude to Jeremiel for his wisdom!*

## Experiment (Group Adaptation)

***Please consider that the following experiment is highly personal and requires the honour, integrity and confidentiality of an angel. Everything that is shared with your partner is in strict confidence, and must stay between you both forever. It is a privilege to be given a glimpse into another's soul. Honour and respect that.***

*Ready to BE an angel? Here's your chance! Choose a partner. For the next 20 minutes, you and your partner will be Forgiveness Angels to one another. Find a private spot in the room. Decide who will be an Angel and who will be a human first. When you've chosen, begin by both closing your eyes and breathing deeply, calling in Jeremiel to guide the process. For the Angel, set the intention that Jeremiel open your heart space, and help you hold non-judgmental, loving, compassionate space for your partner. For the Human, set the intention that Jeremiel open your heart space, and help you be honest with your partner, and yourself, and receive healing release for your highest and best.*

*When ready, open your eyes. The Human now tells their angel all the perceived terrible, horrible, rotten, no good, very bad deeds they have done, things they are ashamed of, not proud of, or feel unworthy of feeling. After the human makes each statement of honesty, the Angel sincerely and compassionately says: I FORGIVE YOU.*

*After 10 minutes, switch roles. Reconnect with Jeremiel and set the intention that fits your role. Repeat the experiment for your partner.*

*When the experiment is over, thank your angel. Take a moment to reflect on this experience in your journal. Do you feel forgivable? Do you feel a release of any kind – physical, emotional, mental or spiritual? If you wish, write a reminder statement to yourself: I AM FORGIVEN. I FORGIVE MYSELF. I AM WORTHY. I AM LOVED. How did AA Jeremiel show up for you? What did he have to share? Take time now to express gratitude to Jeremiel for his wisdom!*

## Feathers of Wisdom

Not only is Jeremiel the Forgiveness Angel, helping release any anger, hurt and resentment bottled inside us against ourselves and others, he is a gift-giver of prophetic dreams and visions! Amaze-balls!

*Try this*: When you prepare for bed tonight, ask Jeremiel to give you a glimpse into your next day or week, always for your highest and best, and most advisable for you to know now. Ask him to give you excellent memory recall of the dream or vision, allow you to receive the message clearly & concisely, and make the message tangible and verifiable to you. Then see what happens! (You might want to keep a dream journal next to your bed for the next week or two. You may not receive anything the first night, but know it is on its way, and you'll want to be prepared!) The more often you call on him for this purpose, the more profound and helpful the visions and dreams will be!

If you are like me, a person who already receives prophetic dreams and visions, and you don't know what to do about them, or they come through in an overwhelming, disturbing way, consider this:

Ask Jeremiel to allow you to experience each dream or vision in a gentle way, so you can be clear about its message, and what you are to do with it. Ask to be an observer, once removed from the intensity of the experience. Your recall will be sharper, and you will gain confidence in your role as the receiver. Trust me…I speak from experience here! ;)

# Archangel Jophiel

Angel of

BEAUTY

Helps with:

- Acknowledging beauty
- Overcoming self-doubt and fear
- Providing perspective - a breath of fresh air
- Providing serene energy

"Beauty is in the eye of the beholder!"

"One person's trash is another's treasure."

"If a tree falls in a forest, and no one is around to hear it, does it make a noise?"

At the core of each of these adages is the concept of PERCEPTION.

We all perceive our world, our reality, in a unique way, influenced by our core beliefs and experiences. Take *Body Dysmorphia* for example. Thousands of women & men of every age with this condition are obsessed with their weight and physical appearance, and see themselves in a completely different way than the rest of the world does. When they look in a mirror, no matter the actual size, shape or feature, their eyes physically see a larger body, wrinkles or undesirable features that really aren't seen by others and don't exist. Their perception of their bodies, their poor self-esteem and harsh self-criticism, however, makes it real to them.

As well, many people who were overweight as children, and lost the weight going into adulthood, carry shame, fear, sadness and negative memories surrounding the experience, and forget that their "now" is different. Their perception of themselves is stuck in the past, often leaving them doubting their abilities, and self worth in all aspects of life, when that is no longer a factor.

Now take a child with a learning disability. If that child is given limitations, repeatedly told that they will never be able to be or do certain things because of their situation, what is their personal perception going to reflect? Will believe the limitations and never strive to reach their full potential? Will they take other's beliefs as a challenge and work harder, faster, longer to adapt, overcome and thrive just to prove they can?

Perception is fluid, not fixed. If you don't feel beautiful, smart, capable or worthy; if you don't like the outcome of your choices; change your perspective and rewrite your story! Make lemonade out of lemons. Ask Archangel Jophiel to help you see the beauty in every situation, obstacle and person (including yourself), and enjoy that breath of fresh air as you shift into your highest truth.

## Intentions*

Close your eyes and connect to your breath. Simply notice the sound of your breath entering and exiting through your nostrils. Feel the breath filling and emptying your lungs. Be calm and deliberate in slowing your breath.
Inhale.....exhale.....inhale...........exhale........... inhale...............exhale. Listen for the sound of silence in the room. Allow yourself to be enveloped by that silence. Allow yourself to feel light and free. You feel so light now, as though you could float like a balloon up through the ceiling and into the sky. As you enjoy this sensation, you become aware of another presence joining you. It is Archangel Jophiel. As she enters your energy, she enhances your serenity and you feel tingly and warm all over. Repeat out loud this intention: Hi Jophiel! I'm honoured to meet you! I want to get to know you better. I'd love to learn about your gifts, and how you communicate with me. I'm ready to receive your guidance. Please show me beauty and confidence in all

its forms in my life, in a tangible, verifiable way now. I'm so grateful you have made it so!

If you wish, take this time now to add a personal intention for this experiment.

Jophiel smiles widely, and leads you even higher into the sky, past the atmosphere and into the universal star space surrounding the Earth. When you are ready to continue your adventure, gently open your eyes.

## *Experiment*

*Grab your hand held mirror. For the next 20 minutes, prepare to see yourself in a new and unique light! Find a quiet spot where you can feel comfortable and have some privacy. Close your eyes for a moment, and connect with your breath. Clear your mind and call in Archangel Jophiel. Ask her to allow you to see your true self clearly through your beautiful heart. Pay attention to how she comes through for you during the experiment. Does she speak to you or share images? Do you feel or sense her presence? What does she show you?*

*When you are ready, gently open your eyes, keeping your gaze soft. Raise your mirror to your face and stare at yourself, as though you are gazing at a magic eye painting or a collage of sorts. If looking directly into your own eyes is really uncomfortable or unnerving, look instead at the bridge or tip of your nose. Resist the urge to blink often, and allow your eyes to see past the mirror image. Relax into the process. It may take quite a few minutes to settle in – stick with it. Be open to whatever comes to you. Don't judge it!*

*Upon completion, take a few minutes to reflect on the experience and record your observations in your journal. What did Jophiel have to share with you about your beautiful self? Do you notice any shifts in your soul's perspective? How did she show up for you? Take time now to express gratitude to Jophiel for her loving wisdom!*

## Experiment*

*Grab your yoga mat, pillow and blanket and find a quiet place to meditate. For the next 20 minutes, you will receive a dose of Archangel Jophiel's spiritual mouthwash – a minty fresh perspective! Clear your mind and call in Jophiel. Ask her to allow you to find the beauty in every situation, and feel the peace that comes with that awareness. Pay attention to how she comes through for you during the experiment. Does she speak to you or share images? Do you feel or sense her presence? What does she show you?*

*Gently close your eyes. Take a moment to choose a colour. It can be any colour at all. You can go with your favourite one or choose the first colour that appears to you. Now bring your attention to your breath. Breathe deeply in through your nose, and out through your mouth. Allow your breath to fill your abdomen, expanding and contracting it gently. As you inhale, give your breath that colour. Imagine it swirling all around the inside of your body, touching each and every area, organ and cell. As you exhale, release any stale or stagnant breath, making room for more colour. Take some time now to do this at your own rhythm*

*You are glowing with your colour now, feeling relaxed and open to explore.*

*Now take a moment to think of a current situation in your life that has you at a crossroads. You may be feeling hopeless that a solution exists, unable to change, foggy, or out of control in your own circumstances. Let's see what joy can be found within this challenge.*

*You find yourself on a beach on the Atlantic Ocean. The sky is overcast, clouds full and heavy with the inevitable rain. Wind whips harshly at your clothes, and you realize you need to find some shelter before the sky unleashes its downpour. You scan your surroundings to see what's around. To your left, you spot a well-worn lighthouse, dull blue in colour, weathered by storms and sands from past times. Curious, you head towards it, hoping to find temporary refuge. You reach the entrance, and enter through a creaky wooden door, into a small opening. Directly in front of you is a spiral staircase, with a loose railing. You follow the staircase with your eyes up to the top of the lighthouse, and see a small flickering flame of light through the slats, beckoning you upward. You decide to ascend to view the storm from the summit, and begin your circular climb.*

*As you reach the top, you see a large telescope pointing out over the water. A sign on the wall next to it reads: Take a glance and see your life, then take another and see the truth. You are compelled to follow this quaint instruction. You walk to the brass telescope, adjust its height to your eye level, and peer in. As you scan the ocean, you come upon a small, simple island, made of sand and rock. On this island, you see your crossroads playing out in front of you, exactly as it is. What does it look like? Who is there? What events are taking place? How are you feeling as you watch it unfold? Take a moment to simply observe the situation, without changing it.*

*You step back from the telescope to reflect and notice an attachment piece at the end of the lens that wasn't there before - a kaleidoscopic filter. This filter is infused with many beautiful colours, and intuitively, you know it provides a change in perception, coaxing soul clarity from within. You flip the kaleidoscope lens into place and view the island – your crossroads – now as an observer, as though you are a passerby catching a glimpse into a stranger's life.*

*What is the first colour, or grouping of colours, you see this scene through? What do you observe through this colour? How does the scene change?*

*Do the people involved change appearance or feel differently? Do you hear any words or phrases that alter your previous observations?*

*Now focus on a different colour or grouping in the kaleidoscope. What do you observe through this colour? How does the scene change?*

*Do the people involved change appearance or feel differently? Do you hear any words or phrases that alter your previous observations?*

*And choose a third colour to witness this scene through the lens. What do you observe? How does the scene change?*

*Do the people involved change appearance or feel differently? Do you hear any words or phrases that alter your previous observations?*

*Take a few moments to review your coloured observations now. Are there any changes you can apply to the unfiltered situation that express a deeper wisdom or understanding? Maybe Surrender, Letting Go, a New Direction or another higher action?*

*After seeing your crossroads through this multi-coloured fractal lens, you recognize that perhaps the unfiltered view is an illusion, a clouded misrepresentation of your truth. The kaleidoscope is the truest view... Every challenge is actually a gift, containing a higher consciousness, a higher purpose, and colourful, creative openings for growth, wrapped up with a bow of joy. Every challenge leads you to an opportunity to experience the joy that is your birthright!*

*You look into the kaleidoscope one last time, and see your heart space come into view. Your heart fills up entirely with the vibrant shades and tones of YOUR joy. Embrace this incredibly powerful experience with gratitude now.*

*Feeling clear and joy-full, you pull away from the telescope and look out the window. The storm has ceased and the sun is now visible in the sky. It is time for you to move forward. You walk back down the spiral staircase, and out onto the beach. A few feet in front of you, half buried in the sand, you see an object. What is it?*

*This object is a gift for you, a talisman of sorts, a reminder to view all challenges through your true lens, so you will always have a joy-full heart. You pick up your gift and carry it with you always, grateful for the clarity and wisdom it represents.*

*This part of our journey is at an end. Take a few deep breaths in and out, moving your fingers and toes, and come back into your body. When you are ready, gently open your eyes, feeling calm, realigned, and joyfully inspired to face your challenges with new eyes.*

*Upon your return, take a few minutes to reflect on your given clarity and record your experience in your journal. How did Archangel Jophiel show up for you? What did she have to share? Take time now to express gratitude to Jophiel for her wisdom!*

## Feathers of Wisdom

My teacher and friend, Elizabeth Rouse, gave me a great analogy for describing what a reading is – Mental Mouthwash: providing a fresh perspective on one's life. Being the analogy freak that I am, I fell in love with this description as it gives an accurate visual on what Inner Guidance is all about! So I've dubbed Jophiel as the Mouthwash (aka. Perspective) Angel! The next time you are inclined to get a reading for guidance, ask Jophiel to pop in and freshen up the message!

Still doubting yourself at work or in your relationships? Having trouble moving forward through your fears into the life you truly desire?

*Try this:* Call on Jophiel to show you the heart of the matter. Now ask yourself: what's the worst that can happen if you move forward? Explore that scenario. Feel, see or contemplate every aspect in depth – the good, the bad, and the ugly. When you are ready, ask Jophiel show you what can happen if you choose to stay put. Explore what you receive. When you are ready, ask Jophiel to now dispel your doubts and fears, replacing them with a beautiful vision of what you *will* experience by taking the risk, and the courage to do so boldly. Whatever you choose, Jophiel's energy will surround you with love!

Feeling like your world is spinning out of control? Looking for a calm moment amidst all your "doing"?

*Try this:* Love Revolution guru Matt Kahn encourages and leads group love chanting, as it promotes self healing (forgiveness, understanding, acceptance, inner peace). As he transmits Divine Transformational Energy, he has his audience repeat "I love you" multiple times, while holding their hands to their heart space. This ritual is extremely peaceful, uplifting and promotes shifts into a more receptive state for self-love. When you need a break, find a private space where you can be alone for a few minutes. Ask Jophiel to transmit those same frequencies as you say "I love you" repeatedly to yourself, smiling gently, and observe your transformation!

Just for fun: Whenever I'm feeling stressed out and need peace but don't have time to ask politely, I take a chapter from Seinfeld's Mr. Kostanza and shout out

"SERENITY NOW" and raise my fist in the air!!! In those moments, I often can't help but laugh at myself, the tension is broken, and serenity comes in a wave. I believe that wave is Jophiel answering my cry. Give it a whirl when time is of the essence and see what comes up!

# Archangel Metatron

## Angel of EMPOWERMENT

Helps with:

- Empowering us to take back, and own, our power
- Being accountable
- Indigo, Crystal, Rainbow kids
- New energy from other realms
- Applying Divine wisdom to daily life

Let's talk about power for a moment. What do you think of when you hear the word? Is it a good association or a bad one for you? Depending on your personal experiences, your perspective on power may be a very different one to your neighbours and friends.

For centuries now, the world has been grossly out of balance through an abuse of patriarchal power. Women have been villainized and deemed unworthy to be in their own power. Men who do not fit into the elite decision makers club, or believe that women are equals, have experienced a societal emasculation of sorts - a revoking of their "man" cards, if you will - punishing them for connecting to their feminine energies. All things Feminine became weak, dirty words.

That imbalance of power has finally started to shift! Equality for all is a hot topic in North America, burning down the old, male dominated, close-minded paradigm, in spite of its pathetic attempts to enforce what no longer serves humanity. We are stronger than ever in our quest for balance. Yet there are so many of us, both women and men, who are fearful of their own power. It's time to embrace our true birthright and step into our power, in every aspect of our lives. Owning our individual power doesn't have to mean losing our feminine touch, becoming harsh and unyielding, or changing our core values (unless we choose to). Introducing ourselves to, and applying the masculine and feminine energies within each and every one of us allows us to become the more balanced, well-rounded, whole expressions of the divine we were born to be. "ENTER Metatron – our Empowerment Champion – STAGE RIGHT!" He is eager to help us rewrite our definition of power and embrace it daily!

## *Intentions**

Close your eyes and connect with your breath. Allow your belly to gently expand with each inhalation. Release your thoughts with every exhalation. Inhale, and exhale. On your next inhale; fill your belly until you are completely full. Feel that sensation of expansion. Feel the power and inner strength that sits at your core, your solar plexus. Take a moment to bathe in that sensation. Now that power begins to rise. Connect that powerful essence to your third eye. Visualize a beautiful indigo light shining like a beacon from your third eye. It reaches out in front of you, swirling and spiraling up to the sky, drawing you with it. You are in the outer atmosphere, and now out into space, accessing universal wisdom in every direction. You feel connected fully to the universe, supported in its vastness. As you overlook the empowering sight before you, a star, as big as the sun comes into view. It dances with a pearlescent energy that is mesmerizing. As you enjoy this spectacle, a beam of energy juts out toward you. On its tail is Archangel Metatron. Repeat out loud this intention: Hi Metatron! I'm honoured to meet you. Please introduce me to your purpose! I am an open vessel, ready to receive your all-encompassing wisdom and am so grateful for your multidimensional energy! Please show me the depth of my own power, my own light, in a tangible, verifiable way now. Thank you for making it so!

If you wish, take this time now to add a personal intention for this experiment.

Metatron offers his hand and invites you to join him on his energy beam. When you are ready to begin, gently open your eyes.

## *Experiment*

*Grab your journal and a pen. For the next 30 minutes, you will embrace your inner Superhero! What IS power and how do you feel about it? Write down a list of words that come to mind when you think of the word. Review your list. Do you have equal amounts of positive aspects and negative ones? Or do you favour a side?*

*Now ask yourself & answer these questions: Can* ***I*** *have power? Am I* ***capable*** *of being powerful? What does it* ***mean to me*** *to be powerful?*

*Here is a list of positive & negative aspects of the word Power. Power is _________.*

| ***Positive*** | ***Negative*** |
|---|---|
| Strength | Domination |
| Alignment | Self Centered |
| Confidence | Cocky |
| Inclusive | Exclusive |
| Flexibility | Rigidity |
| Generous | Greed |
| Support | Lonely |
| Wise | Unyielding |
| Knowledgeable | Shortsighted |
| Facilitating | Dictating |
| Benevolent | Ruthless |
| Being in control | Taking control |

*Compare your list with these words. For any negative words on your list, replace them with their opposite aspect. Keep your positive list handy for this next activity!*

*Choose 3 negative POWER words from your list. One word at a time, fill in the blank and say: I AM _______! while taking a step forward. How do you feel? What do you notice physically, emotionally, or mentally? Do you hear, see or sense anything?*

*Now choose your 3 positive POWER words from your list. One word at a time, fill in the blank and say: I AM __________! while stepping forward. How do you feel? What do you notice physically, emotionally, or mentally? Do you hear, see or sense anything?*

*Take a minute to write down your observations in your journal.*

*Let's connect with Metatron. Stand up tall. Take a big breath in through your nose and stretch your arms all the way up to the sky, lengthening your spine. Release your breath out through your mouth, keeping your chest high. Roll your shoulders back and down. Raise your chin slightly and gaze forward with intention. Ask Metatron to demonstrate through you how it feels when you are in your own personal power now. Be aware of how he comes through for you. Do you hear, see or feel his presence? Are you making movements on your own or do you feel another energy assisting you? Are you using your imagination to create your statements or are you receiving new information?*

*Imagine that you are Wonder Woman or Superman (or any superhero you like). You stand strong and tall, feet a hip width or more apart, very grounded and full of purpose. Maybe you make fists and place them firmly on your hips. Maybe you raise your arms in a triumphant gesture, hands at the sides of your head, elbows bent, reaching for the sun. Maybe you raise only one arm in front of you, elbow bent, flexing your muscles, rocking a fist forward in affirmation. Go with what feels right for you.*

*Now choose a word from your list of positive POWER aspects, perhaps one that felt uncomfortable to say in the previous step. Say: I AM _______ ! And fill in the blank with that word. As you are speaking, take a step forward, maintaining your Superhero stance. Say it loud and proud! How do you feel? What do you notice physically, emotionally, or mentally? Do you hear, see or sense anything?*

*Repeat this sequence for each of your positive POWER words. Be mindful of your physical stance, as well as how you feel after speaking out each of the words. When you've completed your list, take a minute to write down your observations in your journal.*

*One last time, stand normally now, and choose your favourite positive POWER word. Say I AM _______! And step forward while speaking. How do you feel?*

*Take a moment to reflect on this experience in your journal. Did you notice a change in your conviction from each stage of the experiment? Are you feeling more powerful than when you started? How does it feel to stand firmly and confidently in your own personal power? How did Archangel Metatron show up for you? What did he have to share? Take time now to express gratitude to Metatron for his wisdom!*

*Remember – you do yourself and the world a disservice every time you give away your power! You, and you alone, have the choice to be all that you are. Embrace it daily with Metatrons' help!*

## *Experiment*

*Grab your "wise" book, journal and a pen. For the next 20 minutes, let's explore Metatron's tool for quick answers to your Daily Life Questions!*

*Take a moment to come up with 5-10 Daily Life Questions – issues that affect your everyday experience. For example: How can I be more social? What is the best way to find balance in my work routine? How can I find more peace in my home environment?*

*Close your eyes and breathe deeply. Call on AA Metatron and ask him to provide you with clear, concise, practical information now that you can apply to your questions. Pay attention to how Metatron comes through for you. Do you hear, see or feel his answers? Does a word simply come to you without effort? Is your hand guided to write? Or are you using your imagination to fill in the blanks? When you are ready, gently open your eyes.*

*Read your first question out loud to yourself. Grab your "wise" book of choice, and fan, flip or open to a random page. Read the very first word, phrase or sentence that catches your eye. Write it down.*

*Lather, rinse & repeat for all your questions.*

*Now swap "wise" books with someone, or choose a different book, and repeat the experiment.*

*When you are finished, review each piece of guidance. If the message requires more clarification, ask Metatron to expand on it. You can either repeat the book step, or close your eyes, and notice what you see, hear, feel or just know. Write down your observations.*

*Upon completion, take a few minutes to reflect on your given guidance and record your experience in your journal. How did Archangel Metatron show up for you? What did he have to share? Take time now to express gratitude to Metatron for his wisdom!*

## Feathers of Wisdom

Metatron can also be a great help in these ways:

One of Metatron's many talents is his gift of frequency – he's got great vibes! He can help you raise your energy levels high enough to access the many different dimensions & realms available to our consciousness today. Ask Metatron to join you in your meditation practice, and help you open your body, mind and spirit to experience deeper energy, for your highest and best. Then let it roll and see what comes up!

It's all about the kids! Like Kermit the Frog's plight: "It's not easy being green", many of us incarnating during this incredible global shift, can relate. Sub the colour green for Indigo, Crystal, or Rainbow and truer words were never spoken! As an Indigo, I appreciate having a strong energy in my corner while I live my purpose. I also know a few Crystals who've found peace through Metatron's grace, and I know he is waiting to offer support to the crop of Rainbow kids entering the fray in the coming decades. Heck, kids in general, no matter their chosen purpose can benefit from his energy. What kid hasn't experienced the feeling of being different, feeling like they don't belong?! Do a good deed today and pay it forward – send Metatron to a kid in need. He's up to the task!

Feeling a little unworthy or fearful of speaking out and standing up for yourself?

Try this: Embrace your inner Tarzan! Stand tall and breathe fully into your body. Call in Metatron and ask him to help you to tangibly recognize and express your power as you connect to your core. Then focus your attention on your solar plexus area. Breathe into your belly 3-5 times, expanding it out gently a little more each time. Bring your attention to your diaphragm (its that muscle toward the base of your lungs, right below your chest area) and imagine it gently expanding, stretching outside your body with every inhale. Visualize all your wishes, hopes and desires being breathed into it, and it glows with a magical intensity. When you are ready, allow that intensity to build with every deep breath. When you are ready, on your next exhale, release the energy in a strong “ahhhhhhhh” Tarzan style. Make sure your sound comes from your belly & diaphragm. Feel your chest rumble and vibrate with it! If you are so inclined, throw yourself fully into the part and beat your chest with your fists! Let it all out and feel your strength! When you are in your power, throw a high five Metatron’s way for his participation! I guarantee you will have an: “I’m the king of the world” moment!

# Archangel Michael

## Angel of COURAGE

Helps with:

- Courage
- Protection
- Déjà vu
- Giving peace through relief
- Living passionately, boldly, pursuing our dreams & purpose
- Light workers

Fear is a powerful emotion. As author and speaker Marianne Williamson suggests, there are only two emotions: Love and Fear. If you are not experiencing love, then you are experiencing a form of fear. Fear is the greatest human obstacle we face. It stops us from: accepting others as they are, making changes from old paradigms into healthier, more productive systems, collaborating versus competing, healing our planet and ourselves, and choosing happiness through the pursuit of our personal dreams despite "the odds".

When asked what the world needs more of, most people's stock answer is love. What the world really needs right now is COURAGE. Courage to make choices that require trailblazing, risk and uncertainty - "going against the grain" - to effect positive change and move us collectively forward into a happier, harmonious now. We don't lack love. We need to *uncover the Love that we already are*! Peel back and remove the layers of buried, unexposed fears keeping us from realizing our true potential as humans. Instead of making the focus of protection around all our material *things*, we can be brave enough to protect ourselves from the influence of fear invading our personal peace and purpose. Archangel Michael's specialty is to help us step out of our fears and into our personal power. Ask him to help you *be your purpose* and "Boldly go where no one has gone before"!

## Intentions*

Stand on your mat in a Yoga **Mountain Pose****. Adjust your spine in a straight line, up and down, close your eyes and connect with your breath. Relax into this stance. Feel your power center, your solar plexus chakra. Fill that area with your breath, allowing your abdomen to expand and contract fully. Allow the breath to first fill the belly, then the bottom of the lungs, middle of the lungs and top of the lungs. Then slowly release fully, emptying your lungs completely each time. Become your breath. Continue this for 1 - 3 minutes. Now slowly and deliberately, move into **Warrior Pose**,** remaining one with the breath. Feel strong and capable, a true leader, as you ground yourself into the pose. Allow your gaze to radiate power and strength, confident in your stance. As you breathe and are breath simultaneously, you experience a brilliant blue energy filling your space. It is Archangel Michael. Repeat out loud this intention: Hi Michael! I'm honoured to meet you! Please show me what true courage and fearless purpose is for me! I am an open vessel, ready to receive your generous guidance and powerful protection and am so grateful for your unfailing loyalty! Please show me the depth of my own power, and bravery, in a tangible, verifiable way now. Thank you for making it so!

If you wish, take this time now to add a personal intention for this experiment.

Michael's energy fills every cell and every space between those cells with light. You are radiant! Take one last breath in and as you release the breath, release your Warrior Pose. Shake out your limbs, keeping your shoulders back and chest high. When you are ready to begin, sit or lay down on your mat.

**Instructions for Warrior Pose

- Stand in Mountain Pose, with your feet hip-distance apart, arms at your sides. Turn to your left.
- Step your feet wide apart, approximately 4 to 5 feet.
- Turn your right foot out 90 degrees, so your toes are pointing to the top of your yoga mat.
- Pivot your left foot inwards at a 45-degree angle.
- Align your front heel with the arch of your back foot. Keep your pelvis turned toward the front of your mat.
- Press your weight through your left heel. Exhale while you bend your right knee over your right ankle. Your shin should be perpendicular to the floor. Lift through the arches of your feet, while rooting down through your ankles.
- Reach up intentionally through your arms. Expand across your belly, lengthen the sides of your waist, and lift through your chest. Keep your palms and fingers engaged and reaching. Keep your arms parallel, or press your palms together.
- Gently tilt your head back and gaze up at your thumbs. Keep your shoulders dropped away from your ears. Press your shoulder blades firmly inward.
- Press down through the outer edge of your back foot, keeping your back leg straight.
- Hold for up to one minute.
- Release the pose by pressing your weight through your back heel, and straighten your front leg. Lower your arms. Turn to the left, reversing the position of your feet, and repeat for the same length of time on the opposite side.

*Experiment**

*Grab your yoga mat, pillow, blanket (if desired), journal and a pen. For the next 20 minutes, you will be on a journey with Archangel Michael, exploring the power in peace! Find a quiet space in the room. Roll out your yoga mat and get comfortable in a laying down position. Lay your hands at your sides, palms up. Take a moment to think of a current situation in your experience where you do not feel safe, supported or protected. It can be something as small as needing to keep your house locked when you are home during the day. Or as big as having daily anxiety or panic attacks over a project at work or situation with a loved one. Any circumstance where you feel overwhelmed or even paralyzed by "what could be" or "what if".*

*Now close your eyes and connect fully to your breath. Call in Michael and ask him to help you embrace your inner bravery and courage in a tangible, verifiable way now. Pay attention to how he shows up for you. Do you hear, see or feel his presence? Do you see colour or light? Are you using your imagination to tell the story?*

*Keeping your eyes closed, bring the breath to your core, your diaphragm in your solar plexus region. Notice how your abdomen rises and falls gently with the breath. Now feel your breath expanding into your lower back. Notice how your back physically connects to your yoga mat. That breath expands into the full of your back now, connecting gently into the mat. Enjoy the strength and suppleness this connection brings to your core. Allow your breath to expand 360 degrees from the core now, into your left and right sides, filling your arms and legs.*

*And up into your chest, neck and head. Enjoy being surrounded by your own breath, your life force.*

*Visualize yourself standing on a cobblestone street in Europe. The sun is high in the sky and the air smells of a distant memory. You walk along the street, in search of a place to sit. As you stroll, you notice the people around you on the street. At first there are just a few others. Then you notice that the street is getting busier and a bit louder than before. Now as you walk, you have to move aside for others, finding it difficult to walk in a straight path forward. From out of nowhere, you are surrounded by people, being jostled and knocked around, unable to freely move in any direction. The air is heavy and stale. You are afraid of being knocked down and trampled, and don't know what to do. Notice what feelings surface within you as you experience this.*

*From within you, comes a beautiful orb of blue energy. Michael speaks to you: "You are not alone in this. I can show you how to embrace your own power and protect yourself. Will you let me help you?" Relieved, you respond: "Yes please. I am grateful for the guidance."*

*Michael then instructs you: "Stand tall, feet a hip width apart, knees soft yet strong. Imagine you are the trunk of a very old tree, strong in your space, yet flexible with the wind. Touch your hands together and bring them to your heart. Breathe deeply."*

*As you follow his lead, Michael's orb like energy reaches out to you with long ribbons of light, connecting to your solar plexus, heart, throat & third eye chakras. As you connect with him, your body is filled with a cool, invigorating pulse of energy. A large swirling orb forms between these ribbons and expands to surround and encompass your entire physical body. You breathe even deeper into yourself and the energy reaches out far past your physical body, forming a thick, protective layer of silver stardust, impervious to all threats to your peace. You glow brilliantly with this blue-silver energy, feeling bold and confident.*

*Michael says: "Play with your expanded field and notice what happens to the people around you."*

*As you adjust the depth, width, height, colour or feeling of your new armor of energy, what happens to the crowd of people around you? Do they move away? Acknowledge you? Dissolve? Take a minute to explore this now.*

*Recognize your strength and flexibility within this crowd. Are you able to flow with the crowd? Or stand your ground easily within it?*

*You are standing in your own peace, feeling safe, protected, and unencumbered, ready to boldly move forward on your path.*

*Michael says: "Never forget that you have this power with you always and only need to access it. When you are feeling scared, threatened, or unsure of your choices, stand tall, surround yourself with your protective armor and know that I am here with you, ready to fight at your side, and protect you in all ways. I've got your back. I've got you covered. So move confidently along your chosen path and live your purpose boldly. Where in your life do you need a boost - a reminder of your inner bravery and courage? Let's explore it together now."*

*Take a moment now to allow Michael to guide you.*

*Feeling empowered and supported, you thank Michael for sharing his wisdom and strength. His orb light flickers twice and rejoins your energy field, brightening it to a higher glimmering silver luster. When you are ready, open your eyes.*

*Upon completion, take a few minutes to reflect on your experience and record it in your journal. Do you feel supported and protected? Have you accessed that brave, courageous part of yourself? Did you receive insight into your present issues? Are you at peace? How did Archangel Michael show up for you? What did he have to share? Take time now to express gratitude to Michael for his wisdom!*

## *Experiment*

*Grab your crafting kit, blank sword picture**, journal and a pen. For the next 20 minutes, you will be creating your own personal sword of freedom by tuning into Archangel Michael!*

*Now close your eyes and connect fully to your breath. Call in Michael and ask him to help you tap into the signs and symbols that best represent freedom and self-protection for YOU in a tangible, verifiable way now. Pay attention to how he shows up for you. Do you hear, see or feel his presence? Are your hands, or thoughts guided by an unseen force? Do you see colour or light?*

*Are you using your imagination to create? When you are ready, open your eyes.*

*Now take your blank sword and begin to create! You can draw signs and symbols that come to you, or make them using various materials at hand. (ie. Coloured pencils, clay, beads, baubles, dry pasta, yarn, magazine photos)*

*Notice how you are guided to bring your personal freedom to light.*

*When you feel your sword is complete, ask Michael to give your sword a name. Write that name on your sword.*

*Upon completion, take a moment to review each symbol and it's placement on the sword. Are there any themes, concepts or beliefs woven in? (ie. Passion, courage, truth.) Any surprising or unexpected insights? What is the overall personal message of your sword?*

*Now take a few minutes to reflect on your messages and record your experience in your journal. What does the name of your sword mean? Did you receive clarity on how to protect yourself and your freedom in a healthy way? How did Archangel Michael show up for you? What did he have to share? Take time now to express gratitude to Michael for his wisdom!*

***If you wish, I've provided a blank sword picture at the end of this chapter. Feel free to copy it & use it for this experiment.*

## Feathers of Wisdom

Michael is known in Christian circles as the Patron Saint of Police Officers. I've been known to use this little tidbit to my advantage when I'm running late.

*Try this:* The next time you are running late, call on Michael and say: "Please keep this (insert mode of transportation here), and its passengers, safe from any and all incidents and accidents, and let this round trip be law enforcement free!" You'll be surprised at the results. I've actually pulled over a time or two because I thought I was caught speeding, and the officer zoomed past me to ding a fellow driver instead! (Sorry fellow driver…try a shout out to Archangel Michael next time!) Whew!! Thanks Michael!

Familiar with the TV show Scandal? Olivia Pope, Washington's favourite scandal handler's line is "Don't worry…it's handled!" She is Archangel Michael in human form! Whenever you have an issue you don't know how to manage or resolve, call on Michael for help. He'll tell you: "It's handled!" What a great way to surrender into peace!

Experiencing a case of Déjà vu? Check in with Michael to see what his message for you is! Déjà vu is not just a random occurrence. There is valuable information you are being shown. Maybe it's an opportunity to make a different choice. Or the chance to hear something important you missed the first time. Maybe it's a validation that you are on the right path. Whatever it turns out to be, it's a chance to tune in to Michael's unfailing loyalty! Thanks Michael! We are grateful!

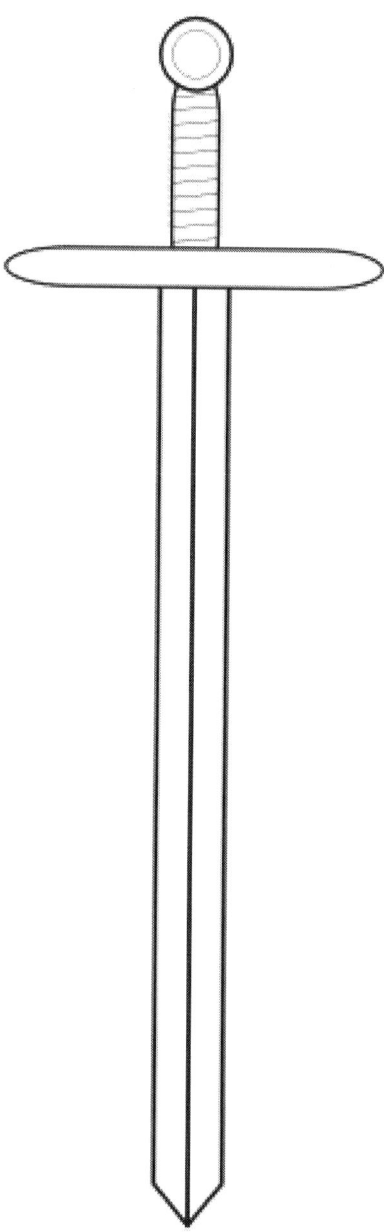

# Archangel Orion

## Angel of ONENESS

Helps with:

- Connection to all that is
- Oneness
- Manifestation
- Co-creation

There is a great deal of material available these days about manifesting. The Law of Attraction by Abraham-Hicks, Wishes Fulfilled by Dr. Wayne Dyer, The Secret by Rhonda Byrne - these famous books only scratch the surface on the subject. When The Secret was released, the world went wild; drunk with the idea of being able to attain all the material, emotional and physical desires we ever dreamed of. It's as though we needed permission to be one of the Have's instead of the Have not's, and it was finally given.

Yet we didn't need anyone's permission to take what has been ours all along. We live in the womb of Universal abundance, literally swimming in a sea of all our needs, right at our fingertips. We either forget that we have fingers and hands, and the free will, to grasp onto them, or hang on to the ridiculous notion of lack - that there isn't enough to go around. We separate ourselves from one another. We separate ourselves from Source.

In this time of shifting energy, now more than ever, we have the ability to manifest whatever we choose, and have it happen in record time. Archangel Orion has come to us at this time to remind us of this inner power and to use it for the highest and best of all. We are One with everything!

## Intentions*

Find a comfortable place to sit or lay quietly. Close your eyes and connect with your breath. Breathe deeply in through your nose and out through your mouth three times. Bring your attention to the crown of your head. Breathe through your crown; the top of your head is an open, unobstructed conduit from the Divine realm to this one. Give your breath a colour, any colour you choose. Watch it fill your body from crown to root, and root to crown. See your coloured breath form a sparkling column from the crown, reaching out to the universe. You and the breath are one. As you stretch out to the vast unknown, you feel a presence connect with your crown. It is Archangel Orion here to meet you! Repeat out loud this intention: I'm honoured to meet you Orion! Please introduce me to your purpose! I am an open vessel, ready to receive your Divine wisdom and am so grateful for your multidimensional energy! Please show me my true heritage and all it entitles me to, in a tangible, verifiable way now. Thank you for making it so!

If you wish, take this time now to add a personal intention for this experiment.

Orion's energy swirls and buzzes around you, excited to begin. When you are ready, gently open your eyes.

## Experiment*

*Grab your yoga mat, pillow, blanket (if desired), journal and a pen. For the next 15 minutes, enjoy a guided visualization that takes you deep into the universe with Archangel Orion!*

*Find a quiet space to lay out your yoga mat and get comfortable. You may sit or lie down, whichever you prefer. Your arms are relaxed by your sides, loose and unobstructed. Close your eyes and connect with your breath. Call in Orion and ask him to help you explore the infinite oneness of all that is, in a tangible, verifiable way now. Pay attention to how he shows up for you. Do you hear, see or feel his presence? Do you see colour or light? Are you using your imagination to tell the story?*

*Notice your breath. Feel the expansion of your lungs as you inhale and exhale. Feel the breath creating space in your throat, mouth and head. Feel that space being created in your abdomen, pelvis, thighs, calves and feet. Spread out your fingers and toes, enjoying the way air feels against the skin between them. Keep those spaces open and free. You are light as a feather. You float up off your mat, through the ceiling, and out into the sky. Enjoying this pleasantness, you float higher still, and reach out past Mother Earth's atmosphere. You are now floating effortlessly among the stars. An unseen current carries you through our solar system, like an unobtrusive tour guide. You gently brush up against each planets atmosphere, and their moons, absorbing all the uniquely powerful energy each contains. Take a moment now to explore those sensations, stopping at planets and moons you are drawn to. What do they have to say to you?*

*Filled with the wondrousness of our solar system, you are curious to see more. You are guided out past Pluto to a darkened moon behind it. There is nothing to see, no stars, no life. As you move closer, a burst of pink, blue, purple and white colour appears in a swirling mass, creating a vacuum within its core. It is a wormhole, leading you out into the unexplored galaxies of the multiverse. With the giddiness of a child, you enter the vacuum, knowing your unseen guide supports you.*

*With the blink of an eye, you are through the wormhole, on the other side, and it is like nothing you've ever experienced. Colours and patterns that don't exist on earth fill your senses. You notice as you breathe in, wisps of white light make up the air. You are breathing in wisps of stardust! With each breath, your body is illuminated more and more with this stardust. It feels so natural, like you've been bathing in this feeling forever. The light in your body increases tenfold; your energy field expands out past its usual boundary. You are the size of a meteor, a moon, a planet, and now a star. You are magnificent! What wisdom are you connected with now in this form that you weren't aware of before? Take a moment to explore your star self now.*

*You explore your life as a star, and become aware of other stars in your proximity. You send your light out in friendship, and it is well received. The other stars extend theirs to you, moving toward your space. One by one, each star joins with your light, adding its distinctiveness into the fold. As each one integrates, you are flooded with memories long forgotten, and you realize they are not separate, merely segments of you! What do your segments have to share with you? Take time to explore these forgotten memories now.*

*These segments are forming a massive grid, a honeycomb of connected brilliance, filling the multiverse to infinity. There is no you and I. There is no separation, no duality. Now all that can be seen, heard and felt is Divine Luminescence. You are that Luminescence! You are All That Is! You are Divine Oneness! What does this mean for you? Does this change your perspective on your life? Take time to envelop yourself in this revelation now!*

*Feeling energized and inspired by reconnecting to your true Divine identity, you are anxious to apply your truth to your life on planet Earth. You detach from the universal honeycomb, leaving a ribbon of light connected, and float back to the wormhole. Your size begins to decrease, but the intensity of your starlight remains. You enter the vacuum and are returned to our solar system. As you return to Earth, vibrating with the heart of the multiverse, with all that is, you are so grateful for the opportunity to live fearlessly. You are Divine Light in this world, free to explore Love in all its forms, knowing you are never, ever alone!*

*When you are ready, bring your attention back to your breath and breathe normally. Stretch out your hands and feet, come back into the room, and gently open your eyes.*

*Upon completion, take a moment to reflect on your experience and record them in your journal. What insights did you receive? How did Archangel Orion show up for you? What did he have to share? Take time now to express gratitude to Orion for reconnecting you to your Divine Truth!*

## Experiment

*Grab your journal and a pen. For the next 20 minutes you will be co-creating a miraculous, entertaining, and illuminating story with Archangel Orion!*

*Find a quiet space where you will not be disturbed. Sit in a comfortable chair with your spine straight, feet flat to the floor, hands in your lap. Close your eyes and breathe deeply, imagining you are sitting in space, surrounded by stars. Call in Archangel Orion and ask him to grace you with the power of connection to access Divine Oneness Consciousness. Ask him to demonstrate true manifestation for you the individual, as well as you, the greater good, in a tangible, verifiable way now. Notice how Orion shows up for you – do you see, hear or feel him? Does an unseen force guide your hand? Do you sense his presence? Or do you complete the experiment using your imagination? Breathe deeply again, and open your eyes.*

*Choose a theme from the list below, (this will be your goal), or make up you own:*

| *Harmony* | *Honour* | *Generosity* | *Love* |
|---|---|---|---|
| *Justice* | *Surrender* | *Truth* | *Grace* |
| *Contemplation* | *Humour* | *Gratitude* | *Bliss* |
| *Sincerity* | *Connection* | *Purity* | *Peace* |
| *Release* | *Support* | | |

*Now choose one sentence from the following list to get started:*

*1/ And then the water splashed her in the face…*
*2/ The engine roared with vigor, eager to get underway…*
*3/ Is that your _______? Can I borrow it? I could really use it to…*
*4/ It's pouring rain out…what are you doing here??*
*5/ Holding a purple brush in his hand, he starts to speak…*

*6/ The melted ice cream oozed out of the end, causing a traffic jam that went on for miles.*
*7/ In the box I found a silver handled letter opener, a stack of $20 bills and a broken wristwatch stopped at 1:34…*
*8/ Sir, can I please see your license, registration and silly putty?*
*9/ When I came to, I found myself on the 50yard line of an empty stadium…*
*10/ The room was completely silent except for the sound of failure…*

*When you have your theme and sentence, get ready to co-create a story with Orion! Grab your journal and pen. You will begin by speaking your sentence out loud. Add your own, fresh sentence, keeping the theme in mind, and record it in your journal. Then invite Orion to add 1-2 sentences, keeping the goal in mind as he contributes. Pay attention to how he communicates with you. Wait and listen, watch, feel for Orion's response. If you wish, you can also hold your pen to paper and allow Orion to speak through automatic writing. When he is finished, build on his sentence, keeping the theme in mind. Repeat this process until your story comes to a natural conclusion, achieving the chosen theme. This can take anywhere from 4 sentences to 30 or more so be patient. Don't overthink your responses! Allow Orion and your intuition to dictate your sentence direction. Enjoy the process of co-creating a story and notice any insights, repeat messages, or similar ideas that present themselves. When you have completed a story, lather, rinse & repeat!*

*Upon completion, take a moment to reflect on your experience and record them in your journal. What did you like about this process? What insights did you receive? How did Archangel Orion show up for you? What did he have to share? Take time now to express gratitude to Orion for his co-creating wisdom!*

## *Experiment**

*Grab your yoga mat, journal and a pen. For the next 15 minutes, you will work together with Orion to collectively manifest for the higher good. Roll out your mat and sit or lay down. Make yourself comfortable. Close your eyes and breathe deeply. Ask Orion to elevate you into Divine Consciousness. Ask him to help you join hearts and crowns with your soul group to manifest co-creatively an experience that allows you to give and receive in a tangible, verifiable way now. Notice how Orion shows up for you - do you see, hear or feel him? Do you sense his presence? Or do you complete the experiment using your imagination?*

*Now bring your attention to the areas of your body making contact with the mat. Feel how supported you are through that connection. Feel the energy from Mother Earth seeping through these areas, weighting you solidly to the ground. Allow this energy to travel up through your body in a wave of light, releasing your high self to float effortlessly above your body, which is safely connected to Mother Earth. Your high self looks around at your surroundings – you are not alone! You are joined by the vibrant, alive, high selves of others also working with Orion. Take a moment to feel the vibrancy of your energy. Explore where you end and another energy begins.*

*Now bring your attention to your heart. Allow it to expand to the edges of your field. You notice multiple beams of light growing out of its center, reaching out and connecting with each energy body's heart within the circle. And bring attention to your crown. Light pours from it like a waterfall, flowing in a rush to all other energy body's crowns, and theirs to yours. You have joined your energy with those around you, creating one continuous circle of light and love. Embrace this connection. Allow it to expand. Feel the endless loop of energy. You are not just your own; you are all energies combined.*

*You have all accessed Divine Consciousness. You are swimming in its sea of universal gifts, all within your reach. As one, take a moment now to seek out within this sea, a $20 bill. When you find one, what does it look like? Is it crisp, fresh and new, or have many hands touched it? What does it smell like? A wave of energy moves the bill closer to you, offering it as a gift. With gratitude, take the bill in your collective hands. How do you feel when you hold it? Take a moment to bless this bill. See it being spent for the highest and best of all, every penny of it increasing exponentially in a boundless supply. What does it feel like to see this money reproducing in generous, loving ways? Take a moment to swim in this feeling now.*

*As one, ask Orion to join you now, and help you collectively manifest the gift of a $20 bill this week, with the intention of paying forward $10 and spending $10 in gratitude for the universe's support. This gift is validation of your own abilities to manifest all your needs, and gratitude from Orion for inviting him to help* *you realize your collective strength within the Divine Conscious. Take a moment to visualize yourself receiving this gift with grace now. Believe it will happen, with every cell of your being.*

*As one, thank Orion, and slowly bring your crown energy back into your own space. Call your heart energy back to you. Allow your high self energy to re-integrate back into your physical body now, retaining the knowledge that you are all one, parts of the whole, stronger together, and never separate. When you are ready, wiggle your fingers and toes and come back into the room.*

*Pay attention to any signs and symbols that lead you to your gift this week. When you receive it, bless the $20 bill. Pay $10 of it forward, and spend $10 with sheer joy and gratitude to Orion and the universe for its unending abundance!*

*Upon completion, take a moment to reflect on your experiences and record them in your journal. Did you enjoy being linked with other people's high selves? What insights did you receive? How did you find the process of manifesting? How did Archangel Orion show up for you? What did he have to share? Take time now to express gratitude to Orion for his guidance and fresh energy!*

## Experiment (Group Adaptation)

*Grab your yoga mat, journal and a pen. For the next 20 minutes you will be co-creating a miraculous, entertaining, and illuminating story with your seminar mates and Archangel Orion! Bring your yoga mat to the center of the room and form a circle. Sit comfortably, cross-legged if you prefer, with your spine straight, hands in your lap. As a group, close your eyes and breathe deeply, imagining you are all sitting in a circle together, in space. Call in Orion and ask him to grace the circle with the power of collaboration to access Divine Oneness Consciousness. Ask him to demonstrate true manifestation for the individual as well as the greater good in a tangible, verifiable way now. Notice how Orion shows up for you – do you see, hear or feel him? Do you sense his presence? Or do you complete the experiment using your imagination? Breathe deeply again, as a group, and open your eyes.*

*Select one person from the group to begin. This person will choose a theme from the list below, (this will be your goal), or make up their own:*

| | | | |
|---|---|---|---|
| *Harmony* | *Honour* | *Generosity* | *Love* |
| *Justice* | *Surrender* | *Truth* | *Grace* |
| *Contemplation* | *Humour* | *Gratitude* | *Bliss* |
| *Sincerity* | *Connection* | *Purity* | *Peace* |
| *Release* | *Support* | | |

*Now the same person chooses one sentence from the following list to get started:*

*1/ And then the water splashed her in the face…*
*2/ The engine roared with vigor, eager to get underway…*
*3/ Is that your _______? Can I borrow it? I could really use it to…*
*4/ It's pouring rain out…what are you doing here??*
*5/ Holding a purple brush in his hand, he starts to speak…*
*6/ The melted ice cream oozed out of the end, causing a traffic jam that went on for miles.*
*7/ In the box I found a silver handled letter opener, a stack of $20 bills and a broken wristwatch stopped at 1:34…*
*8/ Sir, can I please see your license, registration and silly putty?*
*9/ When I came to, I found myself on the 50yard line of an empty stadium…*
*10/ The room was completely silent except for the sound of failure…*

*Once a sentence has been chosen, that person will announce the theme and read the sentence out loud. The person to their left builds on the sentence with their own. They can add 1-2 sentences, keeping the goal in mind as they contribute. When they are finished, the next person to the left builds on this next sentence with their own, and so on, until everyone has had a chance to contribute. If the story you are creating doesn't come to a natural conclusion, achieving the chosen theme by the last person, repeat the circle until it does. Don't overthink your responses! Allow Orion and your intuition to dictate your sentence direction. Enjoy the process of co-creating a story and notice any insights, repeat messages, or similar ideas that present themselves. When you have completed a story, lather, rinse & repeat!*

*Upon completion, take a moment to reflect on your experiences and record them in your journal. What did you notice about this group process? What insights did you receive? How did Archangel Orion show up for you? What did he have to share? Take time now to express gratitude to Orion for his co-creating wisdom!*

## Experiment (Group Adaptation)

*Grab your yoga mat, journal and a pen. For the next 15 minutes, we will work together with Archangel Orion to collectively manifest for the higher good. Remain in your group circle sitting cross-legged, close your eyes and breathe deeply. Ask Orion to elevate you individually, and as a group consciousness as you join hearts and crowns to manifest co-creatively an experience that allows you to give and receive in a tangible, verifiable way now. Notice how Orion shows up for you - do you see, hear or feel him? Do you sense his presence? Or do you complete the experiment using your imagination?*

*Now bring your attention to the areas of your body making contact with the mat. Feel how supported you are through that connection. Feel the energy from Mother Earth seeping through these areas, weighting you solidly to the ground. Allow this energy to travel up through your body in a wave of light, releasing your high self to float effortlessly above your body, which is safely connected to Mother Earth. Your high self looks around at your surroundings – you are not alone! You are joined by the vibrant, alive, high selves of others also working with Orion. Take a moment to feel the vibrancy of your energy. Explore where you end and another energy begins.*

*Now bring your attention to your heart. Allow it to expand to the edges of your field. You notice multiple beams of light growing out of its center, reaching out and connecting with each energy body's heart within the circle. And bring attention to your crown. Light pours from it like a waterfall, flowing in a rush to all other energy body's crowns, and theirs to yours. You have joined your energy with those around you, creating one continuous circle of light and love. Embrace this connection. Allow it to expand. Feel the endless loop of energy. You are not just your own; you are all energies combined.*

*You have all accessed Divine Consciousness. You are swimming in its sea of universal gifts, all within your reach. As one, take a moment now to seek out within this sea, a $20 bill. When you find one, what does it look like? Is it crisp, fresh and new, or have many hands touched it? What does it smell like? A wave of energy moves the bill closer to you, offering it as a gift. With gratitude, take the bill in your collective hands. How do you feel when you hold it? Take a moment to bless this bill. See it being spent for the highest and best of all, every penny of it increasing exponentially in a boundless supply. What does it feel like to see this money reproducing in generous, loving ways? Take a moment to swim in this feeling now.*

*As one, ask Orion to join you now, and help you collectively manifest the gift of a $20 bill this week, with the intention of paying forward $10 and spending $10 in gratitude for the universe's support. This gift is* *validation of your own abilities to manifest all your needs, and gratitude from Orion for inviting him to help you realize your collective strength. Take a moment to visualize yourself receiving this gift with grace now. Believe it will happen, with every cell of your being.*

*As one, thank Orion, and slowly bring your crown energy back into your own space. Call your heart energy back to you. Allow your high self energy to re-integrate back into your physical body now, retaining the knowledge that you are all one, parts of the whole, stronger together, and never separate. When you are ready, wiggle your fingers and toes and come back into the room.*

*Pay attention to any signs and symbols that lead you to your gift this week. When you receive it, bless the $20 bill. Pay $10 of it forward, and spend $10 with sheer joy and gratitude to Orion and the universe for its unending abundance!*

*Upon completion, take a moment to reflect on your experiences and record them in your journal. Did you enjoy being linked with other people's high selves? What insights did you receive? How did you find the process of manifesting? How did Archangel Orion show up for you? What did he have to share? Take time now to express gratitude to Orion for his guidance and fresh energy!*

## Feathers of Wisdom

Orion is a new Archangel energy being shared with our planet during this momentous shift so we are only just beginning to get to know him. The experiences I've had with his wisdom can be summed up in one phrase: Drop the Illusion! While I am already a believer in the idea of this world and its vices being an illusion – a working vacation from my true life - Orion has shown me this on a deeper level. When I'm feeling self doubt, unworthy, sad, unclear, unsure of what's to come, or any other fear based emotion diverting me from my path, I am reminded that we are all one. Everything is perfect exactly the way it unfolds, and every single one of us is playing out a scenario designed to bring us back to our loving truth, our Divinity.

When you are having a fear based moment, *try this:* Call on Orion and ask him to tangibly show you how connected you are to every person, place and object in your realm. Ask for his guidance on surrendering into this truth, embracing your Divine heritage rather than resisting it, which only brings prolonged disconnection and discomfort. Then go for a walk. With everyone you pass, say to your self: I am you, and you are I. Then imagine walking in their shoes, what their day looks like, how they are feeling, what they are thinking. Do the same with any creatures and foliage you pass. Notice what messages Orion has for you through your encounters. I'm confident you will feel more connected by the end of your excursion!

# Archangel Raguel

## Angel of HARMONY

Helps with:

- Harmony & Balance in all things
- Conflict & Challenge resolution
- Importance of relationships
- Justice for everyone's highest good
- Forgiveness

So what does Harmony really mean anyway?
Let's listen to Paul McCartney and Stevie Wonder's definition:

*Ebony and ivory*
*live together in perfect harmony*
*Side by side on my piano keyboard,*
*oh Lord, why don't we?*

*We all know that people are the same wherever you go*
*There is good and bad in ev'ryone*
*We learn to live, when we learn to give*
*Each other what we need to survive, together alive*

*Ebony and ivory live together in perfect harmony*
*Side by side on my piano keyboard, oh Lord why don't we?*

These simple, yet profound lyrics define harmony on multiple levels. On the surface, they are obviously referring to a desire for peace and acceptance despite racial differences. We can extend this to include discrimination of any kind.

Another layer references the good and bad in everyone, the shadow and the light within us all, craving balance internally.

And the third layer highlights that we all have within us what is needed to achieve that harmony, healing others & ourselves. We *need* one another. We are one!

Archangel Raguel is a great resource for exploring these aspects of Harmony in our lives.

## Intentions*

Stand tall. You are a puppet on a string. The string is attached to the crown of your head, reaching all the way up into the universe, keeping your spine straight. The rest of you is very relaxed. Roll your shoulders back and down. Breathe deeply through your nose into your abdomen, allowing the air to gently expand your midsection, creating room for Raguel's energy. Exhale insecurity, instability and indecision out through your mouth, completely emptying your lungs. Repeat this breathing pattern 2 more times. Now ground your dominant foot to the floor, spreading your toes wide, all four corners of the foot connected to the earth. Slowly and deliberately raise the ungrounded foot off the earth an inch or two. Feel solid and balanced. Use your hands and arms to reinforce your balance as needed. Continue to breathe deeply. As you stand tall and strong, your attention is drawn to the crown of your head, by a glistening orb of light. This orb travels down along your spine, leaves your body, and grows in size as it positions itself in front of you. You look directly into the center and see a figure inside. Archangel Raguel has come to meet you! Slowly lower your raised foot, re-center your balance, and repeat out loud this intention: Hi Raguel! I'm honoured to meet you! I want to get to know you better. I'd love to learn about your gifts, and how you communicate with me. I'm ready to receive your guidance. Please connect my mind and heart in tandem so I can recognize the miracle of harmony & divine justice in all my relationships, in a tangible, verifiable way now. I'm so grateful you have made it so!

If you wish, take this time now to add a personal intention for this experiment.

Raguel readily agrees and as he invites you to join him, you feel a distinctive hum resonating throughout your body. He is adjusting your personal vibration to receive his messages. When you are ready, gently open your eyes.

## Experiment

*Grab your journal and a pen. For the next 15 minutes, let's find harmony through the written word! Take a moment to think of a situation, conflict or challenge you are currently struggling to resolve. Choose a power word that best describes what you are seeking from your personal issue. ie. Harmony, Justice, Resolution, Closure, Forgiveness. In your journal, write down your word vertically. Invite Archangel Raguel to join you. Ask him to give you a word or statement for each letter that provides clarity and direction on how to make peace with your situation.*

*Example:*
*H -*
*A -*
*R -*
*M -*
*O -*
*N -*
*Y -*

*Close your eyes and connect to your core. Feel, hear or sense all the cells in your body humming in harmony as your vibration rises to receive his guidance. When you are ready, begin with the first letter. Write down the first word or statement that comes to you. When ready, proceed with the next letter, and so on. Pay attention to how Raguel comes through for you – do you hear, see or feel his answers? Does a word simply come to you without effort? Is your hand guided to write? Or are you using your imagination to create your statements?*

*If you have more than one issue you would like guidance on, choose another word and repeat the experiment.*

*Upon completion, take a few minutes to reflect on your messages and record your experience in your journal. Did you receive clarity? Is harmony possible? How did Archangel Raguel show up for you? What did he have to share? Take time now to express gratitude to Raguel for his wisdom!*

## Feathers of Wisdom

Here are other some other ways Raguel's divine help can benefit you:

Trouble with the po-po?! Involved in a legal dispute?

Call on Raguel, your personal Jedi Master, to help your legal team sort the wheat from the chaff and get a swift, fair and just ruling. Ask him to resolve the matter in a fair and just way that benefits everyone's highest and best.

Can't find common ground with custody issues through mediation? Raguel is supportive, compassionate, and offers balance and an opening of everyone's heart to find a working solution for all involved.

Uncomfortable inheritance disagreements? Ask Raguel to smooth the waters between family members, and act as friend and trusted advisor to reveal what is truly important to all involved.

Ridiculous land squabbles between neighbours or HOA's (my personal fav)? Raguel can settle any red tape efficiently and effectively, allowing you to get on with your day!

Remember, we are here to learn how to LOVE each other unconditionally. Raguel is the angel who helps us to focus on, and succeed in, what matters – true connection. He's like a bestie! Relationship with our fellow humans, and all living creatures, is the whole point! So use his wisdom to achieve harmony with the world.

# Archangel Raphael

Angel of

HEALING

Helps with:

- Healing & Healers
- Seeing beyond the illusion of chaos
- Remaining stress free
- Finding lost pets
- Travel
- Memory recall of divine gifts
- Revealing & Dispelling negative thoughts that lead to illness, injury

The human body is truly miraculous! We ingest toxic foods, carry excess weight, work too hard, run a highly stressed timetable, participate in health-threatening sports, avoid regenerative sleep, experiment little, take medications with side effects, and often refuse to take necessary mental breaks, among a multitude of other unhealthy choices. Yet our bodies stay the course as best they can. As a part of the global shift we are in, more concern and attention is being paid to overall health and wellness. People are finding more and more that traditional medicines are only a Band-Aid, dealing with symptoms, while leaving the root causes a mystery. This is finally making room again for the ancient knowledge of energy healing – boosting the body's natural healing tendencies with Mother Nature's medicine & the power of Divinely channeled healing Light Energy.

By reacquainting ourselves with our innate healing abilities, we provide much needed support to our bodies. And a little goes a long way! If you've ever done a detoxifying eating program, removed sugar or gluten from your daily intake, or took a much needed "me" day, you know what I mean. After the initial withdrawal phase, you feel *so much better*, physically, mentally, emotionally and spiritually. Those weird aches and pains lessen or disappear, your chronic IBS is a thing of the past, and your moodiness and irritability subsides! And the space you make by eliminating these toxins allows for a higher energy frequency to permanently live in your body. This means consistent, sustainable, higher energy healing. Who doesn't want to feel well all the time?! As the saying goes: Without your health, you have nothing. Archangel Raphael desires nothing more than to help us regain and maintain our ultimate health!

## Intentions*

Close your eyes and connect with your breath. Take five nice, deep breaths in through your nose and out through your mouth. Inhale, Exhale, Inhale, Exhale, Inhale, Exhale, Inhale, and Exhale. Good. Visualize yourself in a very old forest. Bring your attention to the bottoms of your feet. Imagine that you are a tall, redwood tree, solid and wise. Your roots are growing out of the bottoms of your feet, stretching down through the floor, through the foundation, growing wider now, passing though the earth, passing through rocky layers of stone and silt, growing thicker and stronger, rooting you firmly to where you are sitting. The roots become entwined now and form a single grouping that reaches all the way to the core of the earth...the lifeblood of our planet. Breathe now as if you are breathing through the bottoms of your feet. Breathe in the earth's beautiful healing green lifeblood up through your feet and ankles. Feel them tingling with warmth; see them glowing with soothing green life force. Now breathe this lifeblood into your calves & thighs. Your legs now feel comfortably weighted to your chair. This healing light continues up through your navel and into your chest cavity. Now breathe in the green light into your lungs. Let it absorb into all your organs with its powerful energy. Let it warm your lower back...upper back...follow it down your arms, and up again, leaving that tingling feeling all throughout your body. See the soft green glow swirl around your neck, face and head, enveloping every part of your body now in the rooted, stable essence of the Earth. As you stand in this lush green glow, the tree next to you becomes animated, swaying its branches in your direction. You take a closer look and realize that your neighbor is Archangel Raphael! Repeat out loud this intention: I'm honoured to meet you Raphael! Please introduce me to your healing skills! I am an open vessel, ready to receive your all-encompassing wisdom and am so grateful for your unending patience and generous energy! Please show me the depth of my own healing power, my own light, in a tangible, verifiable way now. Thank you for making it so!

If you wish, take this time now to add a personal intention for this experiment.

Raphael's leaves blend with yours as he brings you close. When you are ready to begin, gently open your eyes.

## Experiment*

*Grab your journal and a pen. For the next 10 minutes, let's explore Raphael's healing using the Divine Colander! (Great for times when you are feeling overwhelmed by fear!) Gently close your eyes and breathe deeply. Lay your palms face up in your lap. Call in Raphael and ask him to remove all fear, negative emotions, physical ailments and general ickiness. Allow him to initiate healing in a tangible, verifiable way now. Notice how he comes through for you. Does he speak to you or share images? Do you feel or sense his presence? Are you guided to specific areas of your body? What does he show you?*

*Now imagine a pasta colander large enough to stand in. You can make it with bright white light or give it any colour you feel compelled to. Place the colander on the floor beneath you, step in, and pull it up your body slowly, stopping at any area of your body that you intuitively need to. Allow the colander to act as a filter, gathering any ickiness, pain or negativity it may discover. Continue the process until you've pulled the colander over your head.*

*When you've reached the top of your head, step to the side of your colander, and examine what has been gathered. Do you see specific objects, items or colours? Do you get a feeling or a sense about what is in there? Any surprises or revelations?*

*When you've examined all the contents, ask Raphael to transmute them into a bunch of loving, healing energy butterflies or birds, and release them into the earth to seek out those in need.*

*Repeat this process two more times, or until the colander comes through clean!*

*How do you feel? When you are ready, gently open your eyes.*

*When you are complete, take a moment to reflect on your experience and record it in your journal. Notice how you feel after removing excess gunk from your physical, mental, emotional & spiritual systems. What did you see each time you examined the colander? Did you receive clarity, guidance and healing through the process? How did AA Raphael show up for you? What did he have to share? Take time now to express gratitude to Raphael for his wisdom!*

## Experiment*

*Grab your yoga mat, journal and a pen. For the next 20 minutes, you will be offering self-healing energy to your mental, emotional and physical body. Find a quiet space to roll out your mat. Start by sitting cross-legged, palms up in your lap. Gently close your eyes and connect to your breath. Ask Raphael to help you tap into the vast flow of Divine Consciousness where your ancient wisdom memories rest. Ask him to bring chaos to order through his healing guidance in a clear, tangible and verifiable way now. Pay attention to how he shows up for you. Do you see, hear or feel his guidance? Do you sense an energy other than your own? Are your hands guided by an unseen force? Or are you using your imagination to complete the experiment?*

*Now with your eyes closed, bring your hands in front of your solar plexus chakra. Cup them together, leaving a tennis ball shaped space between them. Bring your attention to that space. What does it feel like? Perhaps warm or cool, empty or full, confining or expansive, moving or still?*

*Take a moment to shrink yourself down to the size of a bee and fly into that space. What do you notice? Has it changed or stayed the same?*

*Now return slowly to your regular size. Give the energy ball in your hand a colour. One half inch at a time, smoothly pull your hands apart, keeping them cupped and rounded. With each half-inch expansion, pause and take stock. What do you notice about the ball of light in your hand? Does it change colour or shape? How does it feel? What does it want to do, if anything? Continue this process until your hands are as far apart as they want to be, while maintaining the light ball.*

*When you have reached your comfortable light ball threshold, gently guide the energy up above your head, maintaining its shape. Slowly lower your light ball to cover your head and facial area. Pause here for 15-30 seconds, or as intuitively guided. Then slowly bring your hands in to the sides of your face, at the temples, keeping your hands cupped. Pause here for 1-2 minutes, or as intuitively guided.*

*Gently expand your light ball back out to its threshold, and lower down to your heart center. Pause here for 15-30 seconds, or as intuitively guided. Then slowly bring your hands in over your heart, keeping them cupped. Pause here for 1-2 minutes, or as intuitively guided.*

*Gently expand that light ball back out to its threshold, and lower down to your solar plexus/abdomen area. Pause here for 15-30 seconds, or as intuitively guided. Then slowly bring your hands to your abdomen, keeping them cupped. Pause here for 1-2 minutes, or as intuitively guided.*

*Gently expand your light ball back out to its threshold, and lower it down to your hip area. Pause here for 15-30 seconds, or as intuitively guided. Then slowly bring your hands to your hips, keeping them cupped. Pause here for 1-2 minutes, or as intuitively guided.*

*Gently expand your light ball back out to its threshold, and lower it down to the sides of your knees. Pause here for 15-30 seconds, or as intuitively guided. Then slowly bring your hands to your knees, keeping them cupped. Pause here for 1-2 minutes, or as intuitively guided.*

*Gently expand your light ball back out to its threshold, and lower it down to the sides of your feet. Pause here for 15-30 seconds, or as intuitively guided. Then slowly bring your hands to your feet, keeping them cupped. Pause here for 1-2 minutes, or as intuitively guided.*

*Gently expand your light ball back out to its threshold. In one sweeping movement, draw up your light through your body from feet to head, and raise your arms in a "Y", releasing the cupped hands. Tilt your head slightly to the sky. Pause here for 15-30 seconds, or as intuitively guided, and breathe deeply. Feel free to smile!*

*When you are ready, bring your hands to your heart and express love and gratitude to yourself for completing this healing.*

*Upon completion, take a few minutes to reflect on your healing journey and record the experience in your journal. How do you feel? Do you notice a difference in your mental, physical or emotional body from the start of this experiment to now? How did Archangel Raphael show up for you? What did he have to share? Take time now to express gratitude to Raphael for his wisdom!*

## Experiment

*Grab your journal, pen, and a cup of tea (with saucer). For the next 20 minutes, you will be seeking Archangel Raphael's message in the chaos of your tealeaves! Sit quietly with your cup of tea. As you drink, call in Raphael to help you bring order to any chaos in your life. Request a clear, concise, tangible message from him through the tealeaves, regarding your next best action towards order. Pay attention to how he shows up for you. Do you see, hear or feel his guidance? Do you sense an energy other than your own? Or are you using your imagination to complete the experiment?*

*Drink the tea fully, leaving no liquid behind in the leaves. When done, flip your cup over onto the saucer, and turn it around three times counterclockwise. Lift the cup and look into the leaves at the bottom. What do you see? Are there images, patterns or numbers in the leaves? Are you hearing a message or getting a feeling about your next action? Anything you DON'T see?*

*Now look at the saucer. What do you see? Are there images, patterns or numbers in the leaves? Are you hearing a message or getting a feeling about your next action? Anything you DON'T see?*

*Upon completion, take a few minutes to reflect on your experience and record it in your journal. Did you receive any insights into your next action steps? How did Archangel Raphael show up for you? What did he have to share? Take time now to express gratitude to Raphael for his wisdom!*

## Feathers of Wisdom

Raphael is considered one of the "big guns" of the Angelic community here to help humanity. This means he has taken on quite a bit of responsibility. Along with healers & healing, he is in charge of pets, lost pets and travel! Let's take them one at a time...

Having issues with your fur babies, feathered or gilled friends?

*Try this:* Ask Raphael for some insight! Use the light ball experiment to scan your beloved critter for any health problems and see what comes up. Or ask Raphael to be an interpreter between you and your pet to resolve miscommunications. "Raphael, please speak to Fluffy's high self, find out why he keeps peeing in my boyfriend's shoes, and pass along his message to me so I can keep the peace!! " Raphael loves to be of service in smoothing communications between animals and their human pets! ;)

Is your pet missing?

*Try this:* Raphael, please bring my beloved Charlie home safe and sound to me now. Let me know where he is and what action steps I need to take now to bring us back together, for our highest and best. Thank you for making it so!

Planning a trip? Driving in bad weather? Or just heading to work? Call on Raphael to guarantee safe, smooth travel!

*Try this:* Hey Raphael! I'm booking travel to Europe. Please protect my ticket purchase, the staff of the airline, my luggage, all transportation and accommodations to, from and in between, as well as myself and my party. Please keep us safe, happy, healthy and whole, and allow us to enjoy the many adventures awaiting us with the joy of a child! And so it is!

*Or this*: Hey Raphael! Traffic is really crazy out here today. Please keep me and my car safe from harm and allow me to arrive at my destination calm, balanced and incident free. Thank you!

*Or this:* Raphael I'm going to be really late!! Please give me a time portal and a law enforcement free zone today to get me where I need to be, on time, and in one piece! Thanks for making it so!

I can personally endorse all of the above suggestions! They work every time!

# Archangel Raziel

Angel of

WISDOM

Helps with:

- Esoteric knowledge, material and wisdom
- Releasing fear of being psychic
- Seeing, knowing, feeling & hearing Divine guidance
- Manifestation, Divine Magic, Alchemy

Knowledge is power. Decisions are made every minute of every day. Some of them are informed and beneficial, most are rushed and fear driven. Without having all the information needed to understand what impact a decision will make, one can feel lost, out of control, incapable, or unworthy. With the Internet, global access to an overwhelming plethora of accurate and inaccurate information on any topic, condition or interest is right at one's fingertips. How does one discern what knowledge is crucial to moving forward successfully in that moment?

Likewise, with the reappearance and re-entry of esoteric metaphysical wisdom from past civilizations to our 3D reality, we are further challenged to interpret and understand the messages within. Our ancestors embedded all the answers. Everything we need to successfully evolve as a human race, to get back on track, to unlock life's mysteries and implement its inherent magic. We follow the breadcrumbs eagerly, but we don't know how to implement what we find! We need a Wizard who can release the spell over our eyes, ears and hearts, and clear a path to understanding. Better yet, we need to unleash our own inner wizard, because we have everything we need within. The adage: K.I.S.S. = Keep It Stupid Simple applies here. Archangel Raziel would love to help us embrace our inner Merlin and do just that – keep it simple!

## *Intentions**

Close your eyes. Take two fingers and place them on your third eye. In a counterclockwise circular motion, move the skin around your third eye area. Breathe deeply and visualize it opening up so wide, it reaches out to the universe, absorbing ancient knowledge at a rapid speed. You expand easily with this remembered information. Your third eye glows with the indigo light of ten stars. Remove your fingers now and enjoy the sensation you've created.

Take two fingers and place them on the top of your head, at the crown. In a clockwise motion, move the skin at the crown area. Breathe deeply and visualize it opening like a submarine hatch. All the ancient wisdom floating with the stars is drawn to your open crown and immediately pours itself into you, filling your crown with a beautiful white light, shimmering with life. You expand even more now with the memory of lives and learning past. Remove your fingers now and enjoy the sensation of both chakras open and working in tandem.

Now take your hands and cross them both over your heart chakra. Visualize a blend of indigo and white light from your crown and third eye chakras forming a direct beam of swirling colour into your heart. Open your heart fully, breathing this light deeply into each chamber and vessel. See the beam of light now as an infinite loop between the three areas.

In the center of this loop, you notice an energy form growing. It gets larger and larger, until it is so big; you are surrounded by it, enveloped in the light. You realize this large energy is Archangel Raziel! Repeat out loud this intention: Hi Raziel! I'm honoured to meet you! I'd love to learn about your gifts, and how you communicate with me. I'm ready to receive the key to my inherent wisdom and knowledge. Please use me as an open conduit from the Divine realm to this one so I can realize fully the wisdom and knowledge locked inside the Collective Conscious, and assimilate it with complete clarity and ease, in a tangible, verifiable way now. I'm so grateful you have made it so!

If you wish, take this time now to add a personal intention for this experiment.

You stand in Raziel's powerful energy, soaking up his helpful, loving intentions. When you are ready to move forward, open your eyes.

## Experiment (has Group component)

***Please consider that the following experiment is highly personal and requires the honour, integrity and confidentiality of an angel. Everything that is shared with your partner is in strict confidence, and must stay between you both forever. It is a privilege to be given a glimpse into another's soul. Honour and respect that.**

*Grab your journal, pen and your "I don't get it!" book. For the next 30 minutes, let's get some expert assistance on understanding esoteric wisdom! Close your eyes. Call on Archangel Raziel to help you connect to his wisdom and knowledge with instant ease and clarity now. Ask to perform this experiment through his eyes. Pay attention to how Raziel shows up for you. Does he show you the answers or whisper them into your ear? Do you get a sense of his presence and just know the answers? Are you allowing your imagination to take over and guide you?*

*Now open your eyes and grab your book. You can choose a specific passage you've previously struggled to grasp, or if the entire book eludes you, you can simply flip to a random page. Read the passage once through, speaking the words out loud. Now step into Raziel's energy, (remember the infinite loop of powerful energy), and read it out loud again through his eyes, with his voice, as you imagine it to be. Take the passage one sentence at a time. What word, image or feeling do you get about each sentence? Write down any insights you receive in your journal.*

*Now repeat the process with a fresh passage. Write down any insights you receive in your journal.*

*Now choose a partner and swap books. Find a private spot in the room. Decide who will channel Raziel first. When you've chosen, begin by both closing your eyes and breathing deeply, calling in Raziel to guide the process. Set the intention to provide a clear, concise explanation of the chosen material that your partner will understand, with Raziel's direct guidance.*

*Now have the first person read their partner's passage, through Raziel's eyes, using his voice, as they imagine it to be.*

*Now take that passage one sentence at a time. What word, image or feeling do you (as Raziel) get about each sentence? Dissect and discuss answers from Raziel and partner and identify any similarities or observations between them. Both partners can record any insights in their journals.*

*After 10 minutes, switch roles. Repeat the experiment for your partner. Both partners can record any insights in their journals.*

*When the experiment is over, thank your partner. Take a moment to reflect on this experience in your journal. Do you have a better understanding of the passage you chose? Did you receive more clarity through channeling Archangel Raziel yourself or through your partner? How did Raziel show up for you? What did he have to share? Take time now to express gratitude to Raziel for his wisdom!*

## *Experiment*

*Grab your journal, pen, and a geometry handout. For the next 10 minutes, you will be exploring the deeply layered meanings within Sacred Geometry! Place the artwork in front of you without looking at it too closely. Now close your eyes and connect with your breath. Call Archangel Raziel in to reveal any secrets hidden in the artwork and help you understand the multifaceted meanings within, in a clear, concise, tangible, verifiable way now. Pay attention to how Raziel shows up for you. Does he give you a visual cue or whisper meanings into your ear? Do you get a sense of his presence and just know the answers? Do you have a story to tell about the picture and its origins? Are you allowing your imagination to take over and guide you?*

*When you are ready, open your eyes and look over the artwork. Notice shapes, patterns, colours, shadings, shadow & light work. Stare deeply into any areas of the picture that draw your eye until your eyes glaze over. Ask the picture to reveal its secrets to you and get lost in the experiment. The message can be one of the ages, for the masses, or a deeply personal one. Whatever the message, the most important question to answer is: What is this piece speaking to me?*

*When you have received the full message, take time to reflect and record the experience in your journal. Was your message a prophetic telling, a story from an earlier time or personal in nature? Maybe the experience was simply about being in the present moment and receiving a boost of energy? How did Archangel Raziel show up for you? What did he have to share? Take time now to express gratitude to Raziel for his assistance in attaining this wisdom!*

## Experiment

*Grab your 4 oz. glass bottle, essential oils, distilled water, alcohol (such as vodka), pourable measuring cups, yoga mat, journal and a pen. For the next 20 minutes, you will explore your inner Potions Master, and manifest a brew to assimilate higher consciousness. Find a quiet place in the room. Roll out your yoga mat and sit comfortably, cross-legged. Close your eyes and breathe deeply in through your nose and out through your mouth. Recall the image and feeling of being in Raziel's infinite looping energy. Invite AA Raziel in to guide your selections so that your potion unlocks (unleashes) your personal power center where instant manifestation occurs, with ease, for your highest and best, in a tangible, verifiable way now. Pay attention to how Raziel shows up for you. Does he give you a visual cue? Do you hear his guidance? Do you just know the right ingredients to add? Is there an unseen force physically guiding your choices? Or are you allowing your imagination to do the work? When you are ready, open your eyes.*

*Lay out your ingredients on a table or counter top. Grab your bottle. Using the measuring cups provided, pour into your bottle 2 oz. of Distilled Water, and 1 oz. alcohol. Now allow your intuition to take over. Add 5 - 20 drops of essential oils provided to your bottle, in any combination you are lead to. What scents will help* ***you*** *access and assimilate higher consciousness? As you add these oils, keep in mind your intention for the potion. Infuse each drop with your own personal desires and gratitude. Once you've made your selections, seal the bottle tightly and shake vigorously to complete the alchemical process. *You may want to write down your recipe in your journal so you can recreate it as needed.*

*Now return to your yoga mat and sit comfortably. Spray yourself a few times with your new brew and quietly meditate, asking Raziel whatever you wish. You can meditate on a general topic like manifestation, mysteries of the universe; you can focus on a situation you need clarity on now; or you can simply be present and allow Raziel to bring you what you need. Be open and aware of sensations, random thoughts and symbolic visions that occur.*

*When you have received your message, record your experience in your journal. How were you guided to choose your oils? Did you feel a difference in your energy or understanding when you applied your potion and meditated? How did AA Raziel show up for you?*

*What did he have to share? Take time now to express gratitude to Raziel for his guidance and wisdom!*

**Note: Please make sure to shake your potion vigorously before each use, as the oils tend to remain on the surface of the mixture!*

## Feathers of Wisdom

Raziel is another "big gun" in the Angelic community and therefore wears many hats for humanity. Along with esoteric wisdom and ancient knowledge, he's in charge of Manifestation, Divine Magic, Alchemy, and not least of all, helping those of us who fear our Psychic abilities. Check out these conversation starters!

Since Raziel is our Wizard Angel, have a little fun with him!

Wanting to manifest your heart's desire but affirmations have gotten stale?

*Try this:* Embrace your inner Merlin, Dumbledore or Harry Potter and make a wand! You can use anything that strikes your fancy – a piece of driftwood, a fallen branch Fido fetched for you in the forest, a cooking spoon, even an old toilet bowl brush will do. (Preferably sanitized, of course!) Decorate it with whatever you have on hand: fabric, ribbon, stickers, beads, flowers, stones, feathers - get creative! Now call on Raziel to focus or channel your energy through your wand, in an entertaining way, bringing Divine Magic into the mix!

Write your desire on a piece of paper. Lay it on a flat surface. Point your wand at it, then "swish and flick" away! Have fun making up your own spells! We tend to receive universal abundance quickly when we are feeling childlike and connected to flow. When you've finished, burn or bury the paper to release its energy into the universe!

Feeling a little nervous about coming out of the Psychic closet to your friends and family? Ask Raziel to help dispel your fears and accept your magic! He has seen the atrocities done to those who chose to access their Divine gifts in the past and is so ready to help us usher in a new era of tolerance and understanding. Use him to overcome the fear of judgment and persecution, and step into your light!

*Try this:* Stand tall and say: Thank you Raziel for having my front, back, sides bottom and top! I am now fearless in using my gifts to be on purpose and help the world!

Breathe deeply three times to activate your request and visualize all fear seeping down through your fingers and toes, back into the earth. See yourself wrapped in a beautiful ball of burgundy light, feeling safe and secure, knowing you are supported completely. Bask in this comforting sensation for as long as you wish. Finish by shaking out your hands and feet. Hug yourself, and thank Raziel for being there when you need him most! Go on about your day lighter and more confident in your path!

# Archangel

# Sandalphon

## Angel of

## WISHES FULFILLED

Helps with:

- Music
- Eliminating spiritual confusion
- Carrying prayers, wishes, desires to Source

Imagine this: You've been fretting over whether to stay with your current significant other or move to a new apartment or house for weeks. While in the shower, or in your car, in the middle of contemplating a choice and its consequences, the radio squawks out a song that is EXACTLY what you need to hear, and leads you to a firm decision!

Or: You've had an extremely difficult day at work. You can't wait to leave the office to crank up your favourite tunes and shout the lyrics and play the steering wheel drums all the way home. Every time you do that, you arrive at your next destination feeling a billion times better than when you left, and have energy to carry on!

Or: While listening to an old playlist from your "hay days", you are flooded with the memories of your first winning tennis championship match, the day you met your best friend, or your first kiss! You feel inspired by those feelings, and reconnect with your true nature!

Or: You wake from a dream with a song in your head!

Or: One of your favourite ways to de-stress is through a night of outrageous karaoke with friends, open mic night with your guitar, or jazzin' it up on your saxophone with the local band. You feel in flow with the universe – creating music feels like an answer to your prayers!

If you've ever experienced one or more of these scenarios, then you've been visited and assisted by Archangel Sandalphon!

## Intentions*

Close your eyes and connect to your breath. Focus on making your breath circular. Inhale deeply through your nose, and when you are ready to exhale, rather than hold your breath at the top before exhaling, immediately release the breath through your nose slowly. Inhale smoothly. Do this a few times until you are comfortably breathing in a circle.

Now on your next exhale, slowly release the breath in a hum. Then immediately inhale, maintaining the circle. Let's do this three times.

And on your next exhale, release the breath with an audible sigh on "ah". Empty your lungs completely. Do this three times. Now breathe normally, feeling connected and serene.

Take a moment to call on Archangel Sandalphon. Repeat out loud this intention: Hi Sandalphon! I invite you to introduce me to your purpose! I open my ears and my heart, all of me, to the wisdom you offer and am so grateful that my prayers are answered, my wishes fulfilled in such a powerful way! Please show me the mysteries layered in music in a tangible, verifiable way now. Thank you for making it so!

If you wish, take this time now to add a personal intention for this experiment.

Breathe deeply in & out. Gently open your eyes.

## *Experiment*

*Grab your journal, pen and two pieces of instrumental music from any genre. For the next 20 minutes, you will be exploring Archangel Sandalphon's voice through song!*

*Sit comfortably in a chair, feet a hip width apart, flat to the floor. Keep your journal and music close by, but don't turn it on yet. Close your eyes and connect to your breath. Listen to the sound your breath makes as it enters and exits your body. Can you make out its rhythm, its melody? Now bring your attention softly to your ears. Notice what sounds fill your space. Isolate a single sound. What is it? Can you feel it as well as hear it? Can you tell what it looks like from its own song? Call in Archangel Sandalphon and ask him to share his voice, his messages for your highest and best, through music in a tangible, verifiable way now. Pay attention to how Sandalphon shows up for you. Do you hear his guidance? Does he show you his lyrics? Does he share or conjure a memory? Is there an unseen force physically guiding your ears and hands? Or are you allowing your imagination to do the work? When you are ready, open your eyes.*

*Now turn on the first instrumental piece. You can close your eyes or keep them open as you listen, whichever you prefer. While listening to the first piece, what is it saying? Write the lyrics you hear! Pay attention to how Sandalphon delivers his message to you. It may be through automatic writing, imagination, or something you just see, hear, or feel. When the song ends, take a couple minutes to finish your lyrics.*

*Now play the second piece. Ask about a personal prayer, request, wish or desire, and write down what guidance or answers Sandalphon has for you. Again, be aware of Sandalphon's communication style – how are you receiving his message? When the song ends, take a couple minutes to finish writing down your message.*

*Upon completion, reflect on your experience and record your observations in your journal. How did Archangel Sandalphon show up for you? What did he have to share? Take time now to express gratitude to Sandalphon for his wisdom!*

## Feathers of Wisdom

Need guidance NOW?

*Try this:* When you need an answer and are in a rush, ask Sandalphon to provide immediate guidance through the radio. Ask him to send you the message through the first thing you hear on the radio! I like to play the game by randomly scanning stations so the message is even more magical when it comes from a station I don't normally listen to!

Or, ask to hear or see the answer on a billboard or in a waiting room or grocery store. Ask him to make the message so obvious it jumps out at you.

Got a song stuck in your head that won't go away?

*Try this:* When you wake from a dream with a song in your head that loops and won't go away, it means something! Pay attention to what lyrics you are hearing on replay. Often the message is obvious. If you need further clarity, look up the lyrics to the entire song. Chances are great that what you seek or need to know is in there. And it's often the only way to make the song stop!!

# Archangel Uriel

Angel of

TRUTH

Helps with:

- Light, truth
- Illuminating situations
- Prophetic warnings, information
- Spiritual understanding; changes of the heart
- Making informed decisions
- Ascension & Enlightenment

The truth will set you free. The Sun Card in the tarot's Major Arcana is often considered a favourable card when presented in a reading. Many readers interpret it as an affirmative answer for directional questions, a green light on a particular subject. While this interpretation is often accurate, the card speaks to a much deeper level needing exploration. I read the Sun card as the card of Truth. The sun's powerful light, when directly shone on an object, situation or person, leaves nothing hidden. It exposes every crevice, crack and flaw and serves it up for examination to those courageous enough to look.

Many people are terrified of the truth. They would rather be lied to with a happy tale than to hear the reality of their situation and face it, head on. Why is that? What are we so afraid of seeing that cause us to choose the illusion over the truth? Many choose it because getting *through* the truth to acceptance is just too much effort. Others choose it to avoid the unknown. They prefer the devil they know, even if that devil causes crippling, stifling grief and pain daily, because something or someone new is unpredictable. And still others choose it because they are afraid of how they will need to change (or not) after their truth is revealed. "I'll be one of *those* people if I do this. People will judge me."

Yet in truth there is power. In truth there is freedom beyond anything the illusory world can offer. When you have all the information, when you understand all the aspects of a given situation, including what part you play in your own life, before making a decision, you empower yourself to move ahead with confidence and a sense of adventure! If you choose to bury your head in the proverbial sand – if you choose the illusion - you give away your power, and leave yourself open to the whims of others. You become a victim. The truth, while often painful to face, will set you free! Archangel Uriel's specialty is illuminating your core truths with a sun-powered spotlight. In a gentle, loving way, he offers perspective and guidance on the way through the illusion and into the exquisite beauty of enlightened freedom!

## Intentions*

Close your eyes and connect with your breath. Breathe in to the count of 4 and out to the count of 6. Inhale.... Exhale. Inhale.... Exhale. Inhale.... Exhale. Imagine you are sitting in darkness, seeking insight and answers. Above you out of the darkness, you see a multitude of bright white ribbons of light streaming down from the universe. The ribbons join into a single large rope of illumination above you. Bring your attention to the crown of your head. Imagine a circular opening the size of a tennis ball receiving these merged light ribbons. The light enters your crown and instantly fills your entire body with iridescent threads, illuminating every single space within your body, leaving nothing hidden. You ARE light. As you bathe in this realization, you are aware of a presence emanating from you. It is Archangel Uriel.

Repeat out loud this intention: Hi Uriel! I'm honoured to meet you! I'd love to learn about truth, and how you communicate that with and through me. I'm ready to receive the key to my own light. Please use me as an open conduit from the Divine realm to this one so I can shine my light on my truth to live on purpose, and be that illumination for others so they may live theirs, in a tangible, verifiable way now. I'm so grateful you have made it so!

If you wish, take this time now to add a personal intention for this experiment.

Uriel's energy glows even brighter, filling you with the vibration of truth. You are ready for his guidance. Now gently open your eyes.

## *Experiment*

*Grab your journal and a pen. For the next 15 minutes, you will explore how to access your core truths with Archangel Uriel's guidance through muscle testing.*

*Take a moment now to write a list of 7-10 questions you would like Divine guidance on. Your questions can be about your day-to-day life, guidance of direction and right action or deeper life mission and purpose.*

*When you are finished, review each of your questions, one at a time, and come up with affirmative statements, using "…for my highest and best", that reflect the heart of the question.*

*For example: "Which job offer is the right one to take – the office environment or the outdoor landscaping position?"*

*The office job is for my highest and best.*

*The landscaping position is for my highest and best.*

*OR*

*"Do I need to take these antibiotics?"*

*These antibiotics will help me heal for my highest and best.*

*OR*

*"My son is avoiding me. Should I confront him or allow him to come to me?"*

*Confronting my son is for my highest and best.*

*Allowing my son to come to me is for my highest and best.*

*When you have your affirmative statements, stretch your body and shake out your arms and legs. Stand tall, like you are a puppet on a string, keeping your spine straight. Roll your shoulders back and down. Make sure your feet are a bit less than a hip width apart, knees sturdy but not locked. Place your arms at your sides, hands dangling loosely. Close your eyes. Call in Uriel and ask him to help access your core truths to guide your next right actions and share related prophetic information, in a tangible, verifiable way now. Notice how Uriel comes through for you. Do you see, hear or feel his answers? Does he show up as a presence in your field? Or are you using your imagination to complete the experiment?*

*Now start with your first question. Maintain a standing position with eyes closed, and clear your mind. Make your first statement out loud. Notice what happens to your body. Do you sway forward, backward, or remain in your neutral standing position? When your body sways forward, your inner guidance, core truth, is giving you a "yes". When your body sways backward, your inner guidance, core truth, is giving you a "no". When your body remains neutral, your inner guidance, core truth, is indicating your question is neither good nor bad, right or wrong, your choice will not be of consequence.*

*When you have an answer, ask Uriel to show you a glimpse of what is to come should you choose to follow it. Breathe deeply and notice what comes. Write your messages down.*

*Repeat the sequence for each of your questions, recording your messages as you go.*

*Upon completion, take a few minutes to reflect on your experience and record it in your journal. Did you receive any insights into your next action steps? How did Archangel Uriel show up for you? What did he have to share? Take time now to express gratitude to Uriel for his wisdom!*

## Experiment*

*Grab a flame retardant container, candle, lighter, blank paper, journal and a pen. (You may choose to conduct this experiment outside, and keep water close by to douse the flame, if necessary.) For the next 15 minutes, experience the helpful clarity of Archangel Uriel's Divine Illumination into the heart of your matters!*

*Find a quiet place to sit in contemplation. Using a blank sheet of paper, write down 3-5 issues in your life currently where confusion is predominant and truth needs to be revealed, either to you or to another. Record all relevant facts, feelings, people, places and objects pertaining to your issues.*

*When you have finished, close your eyes and breathe deeply. Call in Uriel and invite him to illuminate the core truths of your situation to help you make open, honest choices for your highest and best, in a tangible, verifiable way now. Notice how he shows up for you. Do you see, hear or feel him? Are you aware of an otherworldly presence? Or are you completing the experiment using your imagination? Now gently open your eyes.*

*Take your candle and light it, keeping it close to you. Place the flame retardant container close by. Take your paper, filled with your thoughts, and fold it three times. Light the corner of the paper using the candle flame, asking Uriel to transform confusion into truth now. Place the burning paper into the container and watch it burn, with a soft gaze, until it becomes ash.*

*Move your gaze to the candle flame. Stare into the flame, blinking only when absolutely necessary. Notice how the fire dances around the wick. Look at the multiple colours, size and ever-changing shape of the flame in the candle. Become the candle. Become the wick. Become the flame. Breathe in its heat, its light. Feel it fill your lungs. With each breath, allow the heat to seek out all areas of your body that contain hidden truths within your issues. Don't take it over, just be an observer – notice where your breath goes. When your breath pauses, allow it to illuminate that area.*

*Explore each area slowly and deliberately, and ask the following questions as you observe:*

*What am I resisting?*

*What do I need to see to gain true understanding?*

*What is my truth?*

*What is the truth of others involved?*

*What is hidden from my knowledge?*

*What action steps can I take to find peace within my truth?*

*What Divine guidance do I need to receive?*

*When you have received your messages, follow your breath into the next area needing illumination. Repeat this step until all areas have been explored.*

*You are completely warm, full of truth and understanding. Bring your attention back onto the flame. It burns with YOUR truth, YOUR life. Take in one last warm breath and close your eyes. When you are ready, say out loud: "The truth is within me. I AM Truth." Then blow out the candle. Gently open your eyes.*

*Upon completion, take a few minutes to reflect on your experience and record it in your journal. What was revealed to you? How did Archangel Uriel show up for you? What did he have to share? Take time now to express gratitude to Uriel for his wisdom!*

## Feathers of Wisdom

In need of some talk therapy? I have a great recommendation - Uriel is like Frasier, The Psychologist

Angel! Not only does he assist in revealing our deepest truths, he helps us make informed decisions.

*Try this:* When you are faced with a quick decision to make, and you don't have all the facts, call on Uriel. Ask him to send you the means to receive all you need to know, to make the call that is for your highest and best. You'll be amazed at what transpires! You may be suddenly given more time to research the problem, or a person may appear with just the right words you need to move forward confidently. Don't get hung up on the details of how he will provide. Whatever the method, trust that the result will be in your favour!

Following your own path to Enlightenment and stumble occasionally? Uriel is an excellent mentor to those on the fast track! Ascension is in his wheelhouse. Whether it's misunderstood physical symptoms like overactive dreams and insomnia, psychic expansion of your "clairs", or little known (new) modalities peaking your interest, Uriel enjoys guiding you through the various tunnels we create to get us where we need to be.

Thanks for joining me on the journey Uriel! It's nice to know, even though the spiritual path is an individual one, I'm not alone!

Looking for a simple "yes" or "no"? Look no further than Uriel!

*Try this:* Grab a pendulum and invite Uriel in to your Q&A. Ask him to infuse your pendulum with his energy, allowing crystal clear responses. Then center your pendulum, close your eyes, and ask away! You'll be pleased with the efficient results!

# Archangel Zadkiel

## Angel of SURRENDER

Helps with:

- Seeing self & others with mercy, compassion & forgiveness
- Emotional balance
- Transmuting negative experience into love & learning
- Release & surrender of what no longer serves

Let's shift our focus on to two words for a moment: Disappointment and Expectation. If I asked you to list the times you've been let down by a loved one, I'd bet dollars to donuts you would lose count pretty quickly. Where does disappointment come from? Unrealized expectation. When we expect a particular action, behavior or response from another, we set ourselves up for disappointment, and them for failure to please and succeed. There is no guarantee that the other person will **choose** to come through for you in the way you wish. They may do it consciously, perhaps in defiance of feeling controlled. Or they may have the best of intentions, wanting to help you, and unforeseen or unacknowledged obstacles get in the way. Either way, the result is the same. You feel put out, let down, like you don't matter or count, or any other form that disappointment takes.

What is at the core of all this expectation? Control. Yep. Even if you don't consider yourself a particularly controlling personality, you can still run into the ego's need for control disguised as 'victim' from time to time. Here's the (not so) secret…Control is an illusion. We can't make anyone else do, say, or feel anything! The only thing we have 'control' over is our choice to react or respond to what the world presents us. That's it.

So how can we cope with this sometimes icky, sometimes freeing fact? Surrender. Accepting what IS and working with that, rather than ruminating over what should, would, could, be, "if only" circumstances were different. Holding on to "what if's" is a waste of precious energy, keeping you from going with universal flow, and serves only to delay joy. Archangel Zadkiel is the right pair of wings to support you when surrender feels out of reach!

## Intentions*

Sit quietly, with your spine straight, shoulders back and down, feet flat to the floor. Close your eyes and connect with your breath. Just notice how you are breathing, without changing it. Are you breathing through your nose or mouth? Is your breath cool or warm as you inhale? Is your breathing shallow and high or full and low? Just allow whatever your breath is in this moment to 'be".

Repeat silently: I let go. I am surrendered into this moment. I have nowhere to be more important than right here, right now, showing up exactly as I am. (Pause)

I let go. I am surrendered into this moment. I have nowhere to be more important than right here, right now, showing up exactly as I am. (Pause)

I let go. I am surrendered into this moment. I have nowhere to be more important than right here, right now, showing up exactly as I am. (Pause)

As you sit within your Divine light, you become aware of a presence joining you. It is Archangel Zadkiel. Repeat out loud this intention: I'm honoured to meet you Zadkiel! Please introduce me to my compassionate, loving, forgiving nature within! I am an open vessel, ready to receive your guidance on releasing what no longer serves my highest and best. Please show me how to release, transmute and surrender into the peace and joy that I already am, in a tangible, verifiable way now. Thank you for making it so!

If you wish, take this time now to add a personal intention for this experiment.

Zadkiel asks you to take a full, deep breath in, filling your lungs completely. Hold the breath for 3 seconds, then release it in a sigh on "ah". Feel his wings supporting you as you exhale fully and surrender into him. When you are ready to begin, gently open your eyes.

## *Experiment*

*Grab your canvas, painting supplies, journal and a pen. For the next 30 minutes, you will be surrendering control of, and transmuting, what no longer serves you through painting. While you are setting up your canvas and painting supplies, think of 2-3 issues in your life currently that drain you, or absorb precious time. When you have clear examples, gently close your eyes and connect to your breath. Ask Zadkiel to show you what in your life needs releasing, and how to surrender it to make room for emotional balance in a clear, tangible, verifiable way now. Ask him to give you his gift of compassion and forgiveness as you surrender these issues. Pay attention to how he shows up for you. Do you see, hear or feel his guidance? Do you sense an energy other than your own? Does an unseen force guide your hands? Or are you using your imagination to complete the experiment? When you are ready, open your eyes.*

*Now ask Zadkiel to give you a symbol for each issue you've chosen that represents the heart of the matter, and paint them. While you are painting, allow all feelings you experience when absorbed in this issue to leave you, and enter the brush (or your finger). What you resist persists. Hold nothing back. Whatever comes up for you, in whatever way it comes, allow. If you find you are struggling, step back for a moment and be an observer in the process. Watch thoughts float by, tears flow, anger crest – any expression as it shows up to be loved and released is acceptable. Imagine every last ounce of your emotions being cleared from you, leaving cavernous space within. When your symbols have been completed, put down your brush and take a moment to sit with this emptiness. You can close your eyes or leave them open. Adjust your posture to ground and align your body to the Divine. Be.*

*When you are ready, pick up your brush and paint a background for your symbols. This time, as you paint, ask Zadkiel to fill your space with love, compassion, forgiveness and joy. Allow these feelings to enter the brush, transmuting and transforming all feelings no longer needed into a loving fresh perspective. Feel the fresh energy flow through the brush onto the canvas, and enjoy a lifting of your energy as it occurs. When you are complete, hold your canvas (or if it is still wet, hold your hands up close to the canvas) and infuse it with what you wish for yourself moving forward. Generate feelings of love, joy, bliss, success, or any other that suits you. Visualize the canvas absorbing them, emanating your light.*

*When you are finished, take your canvas and gift it to someone! You are paying forward and giving back the loving guidance and wisdom Zadkiel shared with you!*

*Take a few minutes to reflect on your insights and record your experience in your journal. Do you feel more in balance? What did emptiness, the absence of that which no longer serves, feel like for you? What was the experience of transmutation like? How did Archangel Zadkiel show up for you? What did he have to share? Take time now to express gratitude to Zadkiel for his wisdom!*

## *Experiment*

*Grab your favourite oracle deck (I recommend Alana Fairchild or Kyle Gray), journal and a pen. For the next 20 minutes, explore Archangel Zadkiel's personal messages of love, compassion, mercy and forgiveness for you.*

*Find a private spot in the room, lay out your yoga mat and sit comfortably. Shuffle your oracle cards while calling in Zadkiel. Ask him to reveal the areas of your life that need review and adjustment, and help you realign for your highest and best with a loving heart and a gentle tongue. Request that the review be a positive, constructive learning experience that right action be revealed in a clear, tangible, verifiable way now. Notice how Zadkiel shows up for you. Do you see, hear or feel his guidance? Do you sense an energy other than your own? Does an unseen force guide your hands?*

*Now lay them out in front of you, face down fan style. You will be drawing 15 cards, each with a prompt question. With each prompt, pull the card and lay it face down making a heart shape from right to left in the following order:*

*Prompt Questions:*

1. *What aspect of yourself are you hiding from that needs acknowledgement and release?*
2. *What aspect of yourself are you in conflict with?*
3. *How can you resolve the conflict?*
4. *What core belief(s) no longer serves you at this time and needs dissolving? (If more than one, pull a card for each belief and lay them on top of the first card.)*
5. *Where have you come from? Who were you then?*
6. *Where are you now? Who are you now?*
7. *Where are you going? Who are you becoming?*
8. *What aspect of your past needs your forgiveness?*
9. *What action steps can you take to be compassion?*
10. *Where in your life can you apply mercy instead of resentment, anger or vengeance?*
11. *Where in your life can you apply acceptance instead of expectance?*
12. *How can you best apply gratitude to your life?*
13. *What can you apply to achieve balance?*
14. *What is your life purpose or mission? What are you here to explore?*
15. *Divine Guidance – Zadkiel's Loving Motivation*

*When all cards have been pulled, flip each card over in order and receive Zadkiel's direct guidance. You can read from the Oracle deck booklet or intuitively receive the messages.*

*When you are complete, take a moment to reflect on your messages and record your experience in your journal. What did you learn about yourself? Did you receive fresh insight into your life choices? Did you get validation for your path or a new direction to take? Do you have a clear understanding of compassion, mercy and forgiveness in your life? How did Archangel Zadkiel show up for you? What did he have to share? Take time now to express gratitude to Zadkiel for his loving clarity and wisdom!*

## Feathers of Wisdom

Zadkiel has many different ways of releasing and transmuting the energies in the world!

*Try this:* Take a crystal or an object of personal importance that no longer serves your highest and best. In a loving way, acknowledge all that it has done for you; then release it back to Mother Earth to be transmuted into a new positive energy and go where it's needed most. You can bury the object, burn it, or throw it into a body of water (as long as it is non-toxic, biodegradable and won't harm any critters). You can also give it away to someone who can use it. By doing this, you are making room for more joy to pour into your life!

*Try this:* After every reading I do, I offer up a grouping of blue butterflies to my Divine Dream Team in gratitude for their guidance. I always ask that the butterflies go out into the world and transmute all fear into peace and love for all hearts, and that each person tangibly experience that transmutation as it happens. Feel free to have some fun and modify this to what suits you! Let's make Zadkiel proud!

# Archangel Zaphkiel

Angel of

PASSION

Helps with:

- Sacred lovers, Sacred loving
- Sensuality, Creativity, Self Expression
- Compassion
- Romance, Surrender, Ecstasy
- SEX!

**"Let's Get It On"**

I've been really tryin', baby
Tryin' to hold back these feeling for so long
And if you feel, like I feel baby
Then come on, oh come on

Let's get it on, oh baby
Lets get it on, let's love baby
Let's get it on, sugar
Let's get it on, whoa

We're all sensitive people
With so much to give, understand me sugar
Since we got to be here
Let's live, I love you

There's nothin' wrong with me
Lovin' you, baby love, love
And givin' yourself to me can never be wrong
If the love is true, oh baby

Don't you know how sweet and wonderful life can be?
I'm askin' you baby to get it on with me, oh oh
I ain't gonna worry, I ain't gonna push
I won't push you baby
So come on, come on, come on, come on baby
Stop beatin' round the bush, hey

Let's get it on, let's get it on
You know what I'm talkin' 'bout
Come on baby, let your love come out
If you believe in love
Let's get it on, let's get it on baby
This minute, oh yeah let's get it on
Please, let's get it on
I know you know what I been dreamin' of, don't you

baby?
My whole body makes that feelin' of love, I'm happy
I ain't gonna worry, no I ain't gonna push
I won't push you baby, woo
Come on, come on, come on, come on darling
Stop beatin' round the bush, hey
Oh, gonna get it on, threatin' you, baby
I wanna get it on
You don't have to worry that it's wrong
If the spirit moves you
Let me groove you good
Let your love come down
Oh, get it on, come on baby
Do you know the meaning?
I've been sanctified, hey hey
Girl, you give me good feeling
So good somethin' like sanctified
Oh dear I, baby
Nothing wrong with love
If you want to love me just let your self go
Oh baby, let's get it on

Marvin Gaye had it right when he recorded this song so many years ago. There is nothing wrong with passion, intimacy and sex – either with yourself, someone you connect to, or just for sex's sake! For far too long, we have lived under the judgmental thumb of religious movements, outdated societal "norms", and misguided, repressed humans who've convinced the masses that denying our natural sexuality is the only way to be moral and good. It is time to shed these antiquated, and quite frankly, harmful, notions about what are right and wrong, good and bad, with our sexual desires. There is NOTHING bad about sex. If you want to explore, have at it! As long as you have consenting partners, no shame is required. It is time to surrender to our true passionate nature and enjoy all the joy and ecstasy sensual, sexual encounters provide. There's a reason why orgasms alter our energetic states. Sex is meant to raise our vibrations, adjust our frequencies, to support the elevated paths we chose to pursue in this lifetime. And it's meant to be fun! So let's peel off our shame, guilt and shy suits, replace them with our birthday suits, and follow Marvin's lead – Oh baby, let's get it on! And just as there's an app for that, there's also an Archangel for that! Meet Zaphkiel, the Angel of Passion!

## *Intentions**

Close your eyes. Sit in stillness for a moment. Bring attention to your heart. Feel it beating in your chest. Notice its rhythm and speed. Match your breath to your heartbeat. Now bring attention to your sacral chakra. Notice its rhythm and speed. Listen closely. Can you hear its voice yearning to be heard? Can you feel its subtle pulse pulling you toward your desires? Lean into that feeling now. Notice how it feels to move into your desires, the expressive freedom that comes to you in a rush! As you enjoy this connection, a warm glow begins to form below your navel. It spreads slowly to permeate your entire midsection and pelvic area. Any unrealized, unexplored passions inside you are rising through this glow. You sense a presence joining these passions, an inspiring wellspring of sacred expression. It is Archangel Zaphkiel!

Repeat out loud this intention: I'm honoured to meet you Zaphkiel! I am an open vessel, ready to learn how to access my inner sacred lover and am so grateful for your unending passionate energy! Please show me the depth of my own passion, my own sensuality, in a tangible, verifiable way now. Thank you for making it so!

If you wish, take this time now to add a personal intention for this experiment.

Zaphkiel's energy spreads throughout your entire body now, and you are filled with anticipation! When you are ready, gently open your eyes.

## Experiment*

*Grab your yoga mat, pillow, blanket (if desired), mood music (I recommend Chill Out Radio on Pandora), journal and a pen. For the next 20 minutes, let's get lost in the shimmering blending line between sensuality and sexual desire through a guided fantasy meditation with Madame Feather and Archangel Zaphkiel!*

*Find a private, quiet space to lay out your yoga mat and get comfortable. Turn on your mood music, close your eyes, and connect to your breath. Inhale to the count of three and exhale smoothly, to the count of five. Repeat this breathing for the next minute or two until you feel relaxed. Call in Zaphkiel and ask her to open your heart to the playful delights surrender can bring when you embrace your sensual nature in a tangible, verifiable way now. Pay attention to how Zaphkiel shows up for you. Do you see, hear or feel her presence? Do you sense her light? Does an unseen force guide you? Or are you using your imagination to flow with the experiment? Allow a little smile to show on your face in anticipation of the adventure ahead!*

*Imagine that you are standing in front of large, ornate black lacquered door. It looks freshly painted, and gleams enticingly in the light of the sun behind you. The doorbell is an old fashioned bell hanging from a beautifully designed wrought iron hinge; a velvet red ribbon, tied in a bow hangs at the base of the chain. You reach out and ring the bell, with curious anticipation of what you'll find on the other side of that door. A melodious sound of oriental pan flute chimes fills your ears and the door opens to a beautifully robed woman, adorned with jewels, feathers and frill. "Welcome! I am Madame Feather. I am your host in this palace of sensual pleasures." You walk inside and she closes the door behind you. The large room is gorgeous, romantically lit with one hundred candles. Luxurious fabrics of silk, satin, velvet, lace and chiffon in patterns and colours you never imagined could exist in one place fill the room. Satin swatches dress the walls. Velvet chairs and chaise lounges draped with silk scarves and lace handbags are placed throughout the room at various stations, inviting you to explore what is offered in comfort. Delicate beading and glittering gems add classy finishing touches in every corner.*

*Madame Feather directs you to a gauzy screened divider on the right and invites you to change out of your outfit and into more appropriate attire. Behind the divider is a rack of the richest, finest lingerie in the world - fabrics that feel heavenly to the touch. A rack full of the sexiest Italian shoes sits nestled under an antique table of the most gorgeous necklaces, bracelets and earrings, in every colour you can imagine. Take time now to explore the rack and choose your favourite. How do you feel as you browse the selection? What does it feel like as you put the item on? How does the fabric feel on your skin? How do you feel wearing these luxury items?*

*Dressed luxuriously, you walk out from behind the divider. Madame Feather leads you to a table filled with perfume and cologne bottles of varying shapes and sizes and invites you to sample the scents. You sit in a large, overstuffed boudoir armchair and view these bottles. Some are very ornate, decorated with gold and silver filigree, some are coloured glass or solid metal, others are clear and plain with only a satin tassel and the liquid contained within to distinguish them. Take time now to smell each of them and choose your favourite fragrance. Do you enjoy floral, fruity, earthy or musky scents? Or do you create your own combination? As you take in these aromas, do any positive sensual memories - people, places or objects - come to mind? When you've chosen your favourite and applied it, how do you feel?*

*Smelling delicious, you turn to Madame Feather for your next experience. She takes your arm and walks you across the room to a stunning bar, with a cushioned high top stool, draped in a sheer cover of your favourite colour, patterned with a tailored gold design. On the bar is an array of gold bowls and little velvet pillows, each containing the most delectable culinary treats you've ever seen - chocolates, berries, figs, truffles, candies, fudge; imported olives, oils, and cheeses, caviar. As you take your seat, a beautiful bartender offers you an aperitif of choice. The selection is endless. Take time now to choose your drink and indulge your taste buds. What does each item taste like to you? Do you enjoy their textures and flavours? What does your drink feel like as you let it slide along your tongue, down your throat, and into your core? How does each item make you feel as you eat it?*

*Feeling pleasantly sated, with drink in hand, Madame Feather leads you to a small dance floor in the center of the room, with fancy chairs on either side. A softly lit jukebox stands at the end of the floor, with a bowl of shiny new coins sitting on top of it, guaranteeing an endless playlist! She hands you a black velvet bound book with silver lettering on the spine and cover. It is a detailed list of all your favourite tunes. Take time now to flip through the parchment and select a song or two that heightens or enhances the mood you are in. What genre is your song from? Do you enjoy it by dancing or sitting and listening to the melody? If you are dancing, are you enjoying dancing alone or with a partner of choice? How do you feel when it's playing? What are you feeling physically, mentally and emotionally? Are you turned on?*

*With your favourite songs still playing, you feel excited to experience the next delight that awaits you. Madame Feather guides you off to a curtained corner on the left side of the room. The curtain reminds you of something royalty would use, trimmed with gold and silver roping, thick and rich to the touch. She pulls a drawstring and the curtains part, revealing the most luxurious, opulent boudoir you could have ever imagined. A circular shaped king sized bed dressed in silk sheets and a mountain of overstuffed pillows dazzles your eyes. Strips of flowing lace and organza fabric gather loosely from each corner to the center of the ceiling, where a full crystal chandelier hangs over the bed, warmly highlighting the long stemmed roses and strewn petals on top of the sheets. To the left of the bed, a basket of massage oils, hot stones, long peacock feathers, and other toys sits. To the right of the bed, a Jacuzzi tub filled with bubbles steams up against the floor-to-ceiling mirror on the wall. Egyptian cotton towels and bathrobes lay out on another pretty chair to the side of the tub. Take time now to experience this visual extravagance with your own eyes. When you look around, how do you feel? What are your eyes drawn to first? What is the biggest visual turn on for you? Look at yourself in the mirror. What or who do you see?*

*Madame Feather invites you to step into the boudoir. "I will leave you now in Zaphkiel's energy. If there is anything you need…". As she speaks, she places a tiny bell in your hand, and closes the curtain. Take time now to enjoy this room, as you desire. Ask Zaphkiel to create a new sexual fantasy or recall and relive a previous experience. You can involve a fantasy partner or partners, or explore on your own. Swim in your ecstasy. Anything goes!*

*When you are ready, come back into the room. Stretch your arms and legs and gently open your eyes.*

*Take time to reflect and record the experience in your journal. Did you enjoy surrendering to the sensual delights of the body? Was your sexual fantasy fulfilling? Did it reveal or unlock any hidden desires you weren't previously aware of? Were you able to be present for the entire experiment? How did Archangel Zaphkiel show up for you? What did she have to share? Take time now to express gratitude to Zaphkiel for the pep in your step today through her passionate guidance!*

## Feathers of Wisdom

Archangel Zaphkiel offers her wisdom and guidance in many ways and through many means.

Want to understand your needs better so you can clearly express them with your lover?

*Try this:* The 5 Love Languages by Gary Chapman was released in 1995 and revolutionized romantic relationships for those who read it. It's a game changer. Simply put, the author breaks down personal core needs of each person into 5 categories: Physical Touch, Quality Time, Words of Affirmation, Gifts Received (Given), & Acts of Service. Each primary category represents the way that person receives (and often expresses) love. If you know this secret about yourself and your partner, it's like winning a golden ticket to visit Willy Wonka's Chocolate Factory. Understanding, clarity and open communication lead to deeper intimacy – what a prize! I personally believe Zaphkiel had her wings all over this book inspiration!

If this is your first exposure, or you'd like a refresher, take a minute to check out *www.5LoveLanguages.com* and take their quiz. Allow Zaphkiel to improve your relationship tenfold!

Sacral chakra out of whack? Then Zaphkiel says: Orange is the new black!

*Try this:* Run yourself a hot bath, using orange soap or a citrus orange essential oil, and light orange candles. Soak in the tub for as long as you'd like. Take a loofah (orange if you have one) and gently rub your skin in a circle just below your navel and above your pelvic bone.

Call in Zaphkiel and ask her to clear all blockages in your sacral area. When you feel a shift or release, release the loofah and visualize an orange stream of light filling your sacral area and connecting up to your heart space. Allow Zaphkiel to use this light to infuse you with a surplus of sensual creativity. See, hear and/or feel this energy to your core. When you are finished, sip on a Fuzzy Navel (or a glass of orange juice) to seal the deal!

# What's Next?

I sincerely hope you have enjoyed getting to know the Archangels personally through this creative experiment!

Perhaps you resonated with some more so than others, and need more time to connect.

Maybe you've learned that all of them need to be a part of your Divine Dream Team on the regular.

Or perhaps you realized you've had a relationship with one or more Archangels for some time, but didn't realize exactly who you were communicating with.

Whatever your experience, take what was given as a gift from the Divine. You are free to do with it what you choose.

In my own Archangel Experiment, I discovered a level of effortlessness to my life that I've been striving for since my birth. The comfort and loving care that came *to* me, *through* me, and from *within* me, in spite of my skeptical mind, has shifted me in ways I'm still processing.

My issues have always been around worthiness and self-doubt. Through the creation and completion of these encounters, I experienced trust in my Divine on a level so deep, I uncovered an internal "hum" - my core frequency, my essence. Before my experiment, I often felt like a guest in my own intuition, tapping in for short visits, not wanting to overstay my welcome. Every new visit, I'd be so nervous they might not let me back in! I now live consistently within the Universal flow, knowing that I am not separate from it, nor it from me. Being on a "first name basis" with my Arch's, my *League of Luminaries*, has allowed me to fully accept and embrace ME!

My goal each day is to live with the honour and integrity of an Archangel in all I do, and continue to deepen the relationships I have established with them. I can't wait to see where I grow next!

What will you do with your gift?

You can chalk it up to a cool experience, something you did once.

You can tune in occasionally, as issues arise, knowing you've already made an introduction.

You might feel a connection with certain Archangels and choose to explore those relationships further.

Or maybe the experiment has unlocked a deeper pathway within that you wish to explore fully with the Archangels' help.

Whatever you choose, I challenge you to continue what you started. Develop these Divine relationships on your own, in your own way and pace, and investigate all they can offer for your spiritual growth. Even if you don't feel a connection with a specific archangel now, it is likely your spiritual journey will present a future opportunity to take advantage of their guidance! (I know that has been the case with me.) Knowing how they communicate with you is invaluable when that time comes.

Consider striving to live with the honour and integrity of an Archangel in your daily life as the next great experiment! You now have 18 role models, 18 loving friends, to emulate!

Live long and prosper!

**I Have a Dream**

I have a dream, a song to sing
To help me cope with anything
If you see the wonder of a fairy tale
You can take the future even if you fail
I believe in angels
Something good in everything I see
I believe in angels
When I know the time is right for me
I'll cross the stream – I have a dream

I have a dream, a fantasy
To help me through reality
And my destination makes it worth the while
Pushing through the darkness still another mile
I believe in angels
Something good in everything I see
I believe in angels
When I know the time is right for me
I'll cross the stream – I have a dream
I'll cross the stream – I have a dream

I have a dream, a song to sing
To help me cope with anything
If you see the wonder of a fairy tale
You can take the future even if you fail
I believe in angels
Something good in everything I see
I believe in angels
When I know the time is right for me
I'll cross the stream – I have a dream
I'll cross the stream – I have a dream

~ ABBA

# About the Author

Stacey Brown, The Black Feather Intuitive, has been highly intuitive her entire life. As a child, Divine Spirit came to her through dreams and visions, and a powerful sensitivity to energies, both in people and places. After years of pursuing many creative avenues to fulfill the spiritual yearning in her heart, her psychic abilities found a purpose and place to blossom.

*"As a trained opera singer, I've used my voice to reach and teach kids, teens and adults alike for many years, and now I'm excited to use it in a different capacity: to help heal others! My life purpose is to help others find – and live – their highest and best lives. I'm honoured to help you find* your *truth!"*

In addition to her extensive local and remote Psychic Intuitive work with clients, she is a Certified Empowerment Coach, vlogger of Feathers of Wisdom (YouTube), author of *Teen Superpower IG: Demystify your Inner Guidance using Tarot,* and recording artist of multiple guided meditations including *Creating Your Happy Place* and the popular *Wings* series (available on Amazon & iTunes). She lives in Morrisville, NC with her supportive husband, two beautiful stepdaughters, and two fur babies. Keep you eyes peeled for her webinar: *The Archangel Experiment*, and her 3rd book, the next in the Teen Superpower IG series.

## Other works by The Black Feather Intuitive:

### *Guided Meditations*

(Available on Amazon)

*On Butterfly Wings (Healing)*

*On Bumblebee Wings (Self Awareness)*

*On Phoenix Wings (Transformation)*

*Instant Vacation: Creating Your Happy Place*

*Dream the Magic Within*
*Bedtime Guided Meditation for Kids*

### *Books*

*Teen Superpower IG:*
*Demystify Your Inner Guidance using Tarot*

*Teen Superpower IG:*
*Demystify Your Inner Guidance using Archangels*
*(Available Summer 2017)*

*Teen Superpower IG:*
*Demystify Your Inner Guidance using Meditation*
*(Available Summer 2017)*

### *Webinars & Workshops*

*The Archangel Experiment: Elevate your Relationship with the Divine*
*An In-depth Inspiration for Deepening your Relationship*
*(Available Spring 2017)*

***To schedule a Vision reading or coaching session, contact Stacey directly. (Remote sessions available.) Please visit her web site for contact information and updates.***
**www.blackfeatherintuition.com**

Made in the
USA
Lexington, KY